ESSEX MURDERS

FOUL DEEDS AND SUSPICIOUS DEATHS Series

Foul Deeds and Suspicious Deaths series explores in detail crimes of passion, brutal murders, grisly deeds and foul misdemeanours. From Victorian street crime, to more modern murder where passion, jealousy, or social depravation brought unexpected violence to those involved. From mysterious death to murder and manslaughter, the books are a fascinating insight into not only those whose lives are forever captured by the suffering they endured, but also into the society that moulded and shaped their lives. Each book takes you on a journey into the darker and unknown side of the area.

Other titles in the series

Foul Deeds and Suspicious Deaths in Blackburn & Hyndburn, Steve Greenhalgh
ISBN: 1-903425-18-2

Foul Deeds and Suspicious Deaths in and around Chesterfield, Geoffrey Sadler
ISBN: 1-903425-30-1

Foul Deeds and Suspicious Deaths in & around Durham, Maureen Anderson
ISBN: 1-903425-46-8

Foul Deeds and Suspicious Deaths in and around Halifax, Stephen Wade
ISBN: 1-903425-45-X

Foul Deeds and Suspicious Deaths in Leeds, David Goodman
ISBN: 1-903425-08-5

Foul Deeds and Suspicious Deaths in Nottingham, Kevin Turton
ISBN: 1-903425-35-2

Foul Deeds and Suspicious Deaths in and around Rotherham, Kevin Turton
ISBN: 1-903425-27-1

Foul Deeds and Suspicious Deaths Around the Tees, Maureen Anderson
ISBN: 1-903425-26-3

More Foul Deeds and Suspicious Deaths in Wakefield, Kate Taylor
ISBN: 1-903425-48-4

Foul Deeds and Suspicious Deaths in York, Keith Henson
ISBN: 1-903425-33-6

Foul Deeds and Suspicious Deaths on the Yorkshire Coast, Alan Whitworth
ISBN: 1-903425-01-8

Please contact us via any of the methods below for more information or a catalogue.
WHARNCLIFFE BOOKS
47 Church Street - Barnsley - South Yorkshire - S70 2AS
Tel: 01226 734555 - 734222 Fax: 01226 724438
E-mail: enquiries@pen-and-sword.co.uk - Website: www.wharncliffebooks.co.uk

ESSEX MURDERS

PAUL DONNELLEY

Series Editor
Brian Elliott

Wharncliffe Books

First Published in Great Britain in 2007 by
Wharncliffe Books
an imprint of
Pen and Sword Books Limited,
47 Church Street, Barnsley,
South Yorkshire. S70 2AS

Copyright © Paul Donnelley, 2007

ISBN: 978 1 845630 37 9

The right of Paul Donnelley to be identified as Author of this Work
has been asserted by him in accordance with the Copyright, Designs
and Patents Act, 1988.

A CIP catalogue record of this book is available from the
British Library

Typeset in Plantin and Benguiat by
Pen and Sword Books Ltd

Printed in the United Kingdom by
Biddles Ltd

Pen & Sword Books Ltd incorporates the imprints of
Pen & Sword Aviation, Pen & Sword Maritime,
Pen & Sword Military, Wharncliffe Local History, Pen & Sword Select,
Pen & Sword Military Classics and Leo Cooper.

For a complete list of Pen & Sword titles please contact:
PEN & SWORD BOOKS LIMITED
47 Church Street, Barnsley, South Yorkshire, S70 2AS, England.
E-mail: enquiries@pen-and-sword.co.uk
Website: www.pen-and-sword.co.uk

Contents

Acknowledgements

Thanks to the following for their help with this book: Becky Latchford, the curator of the Essex Police Museum; my former colleague on *The Daily Telegraph*, Bill Stock, for suggesting several cases; Ben Davis of the British Medical Association; Dot Bedenham of Chelmsford Museum; and Tony Church of the Telegraph Media Group library.

Dedication

For Dan and Nicola, with love

Introduction

Essex is a terrific county with much to offer. Essex is the eleventh biggest county in England with the sixth biggest population. This book is not intended to be a guide book to the highways and by-ways of the county in which I was raised. It's a look at the dark side of Essex life – the Essex that the county's tourist boards would rather you not know about. The stories I have chosen cross the spectrum of criminal behaviour and span the centuries. There are tales from the seventeenth century all the way up to the 1960s.

In the book you can read the true story of Dick Turpin; the legend of probably the world's worst hangman, whose brother was sacked from the police force for having sex with a prostitute while on duty; the tale of the man who killed a woman while he was asleep and was found not guilty of murder; the account of a young man who murdered a couple who befriended him because he wanted their money to buy a new suit; there are several tales of jealousy ending in murder and the link between Essex and Jack the Ripper.

Paul Donnelley
31 December 2006

The author can be contacted via his website:
www.pauldonnelley.com

Sources

Bailey, Brian, *Hangmen of England* (W H Allen, 1989).

Berry-Dee, Christopher and Robin Odell, *The Long Drop* (True Crime, 1993).

Eddleston, John J, *The Encyclopaedia of Executions* (Blake, 2002).

Fielding, Steve, *The Hangman's Record Vol 1 1868-1899* (Chancery House: 1994).

Fielding, Steve, *The Hangman's Record Vol 2 1900-1929* (Chancery House, 1995).

Gaute, J H H, and Robin Odell, *The New Murderers' Who's Who* (Harrap, 1989).

Honeycombe, Gordon, *The Murders of the Black Museum* (Hutchinson: London, 1982).

Honeycombe, Gordon, *More Murders of the Black Museum* (Hutchinson: London, 1993).

Johnson, W H, *Essex Tales of Mystery and Murder* (Countryside Books, 2001).

Stockman, Rocky, *The Hangman's Diary* (Headline, 1993).

Storey, Neil R, *A Grim Almanac of Essex* (Sutton, 2005).

Stratman, Linda, *Essex Murders* (Sutton: 2004).

Thurlow, David, *The Essex Triangle* (Robert Hale, 1990).

Weis, René, *Criminal Justice* (Hamish Hamilton, 1988).

Chapter 1

The True History of
Dick Turpin

'That sixpence cost Dick Turpin his life.'

The romantic tale of the highwayman Dick Turpin and his celebrated ride to York on his faithful steed Black Bess is the stuff of legend. Unfortunately, much of what we think we know about Turpin, actually a callous thug, is just that – legend. Many facts are in dispute. In this chapter I have attempted to separate fact from fiction.

John Turpin and Mary Elizabeth Parmenter were both born in about 1675. They married in 1695 and Mary gave birth to six children. After ten years of marriage, Mary gave birth to their son Richard, the fifth child, at the *Blue Bell* inn (later the *Rose and Crown*), Hempstead, near Saffron Walden where his father, formerly a butcher, was publican.

He was baptised on 21 September 1705 at Hempstead. Three years later, his mother died, aged thirty-three. Dick had a standard education and then, when he was sixteen, he became apprentice to a butcher in Whitechapel. It was said that during his apprenticeship, he 'conducted himself in a loose and disorderly manner'.

In 1725 (or possibly 1728), he married Elizabeth (Betty) Millington, a maid. Two years later, Mr and Mrs Richard Turpin moved to Buckhurst Hill and there opened a butcher's shop. The shop did not get its supplies in the usual manner. Turpin began stealing sheep, lamb and cattle from local farmers, which was regarded as so serious an offence in those days that it was punishable by death. Historians have different opinions as to why Turpin became a villain. Some believe it was out of financial necessity but others think he was just a sensation seeker. However it happened, Turpin tired of the mundane life of a butcher and turned to a life of crime. He was caught stealing two oxen from a Mr Giles of Plaistow and fled with customs men hot on his trail. Turpin ran into the depths of the Essex countryside, leaving his wife and butcher's shop behind. For a time, he lived in caves along the coast of East Anglia, and supported himself by robbing the smugglers who operated there. He took up with a twenty-strong gang, led by the blacksmith Samuel Gregory, that stole deer in the royal forest of Epping. Dick Turpin, the name by which he is known to history, was employed as their fence. The authorities more or less ignored the deer rustling until the reward for the gang's capture was increased.

The Gregory Gang (also known as the Essex gang) – which also included Samuel's brothers, Jasper and Jeremy – was notorious around Essex and London. The gang included Thomas Hadfield, Thomas Barnfield, Thomas Rowden, Mary Brazier, John Fielder, Herbert Haines, John Jones, James Parkinson, Joseph Rose, Ned Rust, William Saunders, Humphry Walker, and John Wheeler. Whether through bravado or stupidity they poached royal game. They tried to rob a house at Woodford but the local villagers spotted the attempt and drove them away. The first successful attack was at the house of Mr Strype, an old man who kept a chandler's shop at Watford. The Gregory Gang robbed him of all the money in his possession, but did not threaten him.

On 11 January 1735, Turpin and five of the gang went to the house of Mr Saunders, a rich farmer at Charlton in Kent, at around 7 pm. They burst in and discovered Saunders, with his wife and friends, playing at cards in the parlour. They told the company to stay still and they would come to no harm. They took a silver snuffbox and china worth £100. The maid ran upstairs and shouted for help from the window. The brigands broke in and tied her up before ransacking the rest of the house. They found some mince pies and wine and sat down to eat. As they left, the gang said that if anyone raised the alarm within two hours they would return and kill them all. A week later, they stole eleven guineas, jewels and china from a Mr Sheldon, of Croydon, in Surrey but then with pangs of guilt returned two guineas and apologised for their behaviour.

In that year the Essex Gang became a regular in newspapers. On 8 February 1735 *Read's Weekly Journal* reported:

On Saturday [1 February] night last, about seven o'clock, five rogues entered the house of Widow Shelley at [Traps Hill] Loughton in Essex, having pistols. And threatened to murder the old lady, if she would not tell them where her money lay, which she obstinately refusing for some time, they threatened to lay her across the fire, if she did not instantly tell them, which she would not do. But her son being in the room, and threatened to be murdered, cried out, he would tell them, if they would not murder his mother, and did, whereupon they went upstairs, and took near £100, a silver tankard, and other plate, and all manner of household goods. They afterwards went into the cellar and drank several bottles of ale and wine, and broiled some meat, ate the relicts of a filet of veal. While they were doing this, two of their gang went to Mr Turkles, a farmer, who rents one end of the widow's house, and robbed him of above £20, and then they all went off, taking two of the farmer's horses, to carry off their luggage, the horses were found on Sunday the following morning in Old Street, and stayed about three hours in the house.

Their next target was a farmer near Barking. When he refused to open the door, they broke it down and tied him up, along with his wife, his son-in-law and the maidservant. They stole more than £700 causing Dick to cry out, 'Aye, this will do if it would always be so!' Each of the robbers took £80 each.

On 4 February they robbed Mr Lawrence, of Edgware, Middlesex, after getting drunk in a pub beforehand. They stole silver, china, money and threw a kettle of boiling water over him. One of the gang raped Mr Lawrence's maid. On 7 February, they broke into the house of Mr Francis, a farmer near Mary-le-bone, having first tied up his servant outside. Mrs Francis, her daughter, and the maidservant were tied up and beaten. The gang stole a silver tankard, a medal of Charles I, a gold watch, several gold rings, a considerable sum of money, and a variety of valuable linen and other effects. A reward of £100 was offered.

In February 1735, Turpin and the three Gregory brothers attacked the Earl of Suffolk's servant in Epping Forest and stole his horse valued at £80. A few weeks later, Sir Caesar Child was attacked in the forest by the gang who shot off the tip of his coachman's nose. They stole £25.

On 18 February 1735 three members of the gang were recognised and arrested in the *Punch House*, King Street, Bloomsbury. One of them, John Wheeler, turned informer and on his evidence the authorities captured three further members within the week. Samuel and Jeremy Gregory tried to flee to the Continent, but were captured at Hindhead after robbing Sir John Osborne in order to pay their fare. Of all the gang, only Turpin and Thomas Rowden, a pewterer, were still at large, the rest either being hanged or dying in jail.

Turpin and Rowden stopped robbing remote farmhouses and turned their dubious skills to robbing stagecoaches passing through Epping Forest. They also began highway robbery south of the Thames but their partnership ended in May 1736 when Rowden changed his name to Daniel Crispe and moved to Gloucester, where he was captured and convicted of counterfeiting.

It is at this point of the story that Dick Turpin vanishes from sight. Rumour has it that he went to Holland. In February 1737, the authorities heard that Turpin was intending to return to England and laid a trap at Puckeridge, Hertfordshire. Turpin managed to avoid the ambush but his wife and her friends were captured and sent to Hertford jail, suspected of highway robbery. They were released without charge.

Turpin then took up with Matthew King, 'the Gentleman Highwayman', who at that time was just as infamous as Turpin himself. Captain King, as he was sometimes called, was said to be well-mannered and even flattered his victims.

Turpin and King met on the road towards Cambridge one

night when the former attempted to rob the latter. King burst into a fit of laughter and responded, 'What is this, dog eat dog? Come, come, brother Turpin; if you don't know me, I know you, and shall be glad of your company'. They became friends and partners and established a base located amongst some ancient earthworks within Epping Forest, the remains of an Iron Age fort, now known as Loughton Camp. They also set up another hideaway in an extensive cave system in Epping Forest between the King's Oak and the Loughton Road (a housing development now stands on the site). They could, unseen, watch a particular road, and robbed virtually anyone who passed along it. Even local peddlers started to carry weapons for protection.

One day they rode to Bungay in Suffolk and spotted two girls get paid £14 for corn and Turpin decided to relieve them of the money. King objected, saying it was a pity to rob such pretty girls: but Turpin was obstinate, and stole the money.

On the way home they waylaid Mr Bradele of London and stole his watch, money, and an old mourning ring. Again, a pang of conscience got the better of them and they gave back the ring after Mr Bradele told them that, although its monetary value was small, its sentimental worth was great. Mr Bradele then pushed his chances and asked if he could also keep the watch. King said to Turpin, 'What say ye, Jack? Here seems to be a good honest fellow; shall we let him have the watch?' Turpin replied, 'Do as you please'. King said to the gentleman, 'You must pay six guineas for it: we never sell for more, though the watch should be worth six and thirty'. Mr Bradele promised that the money should be left at the *Dial*, in Birchin Lane.

The pair stole a fine black racehorse called Whitestockings from its owner, a Mr Major. The now-former owner did not take the loss lying down and put wanted posters up around London and Essex. The horse, now named Black Bess by Turpin, was discovered on 2 May 1737 in a stable behind the *Red Lion* in Whitechapel. In the gun battle that followed Turpin escaped but Matthew King was shot and later died of his wounds. King cried out, 'Shoot him, or we are taken' and Turpin fired, and shot his companion, who called out, 'Dick, you have killed me'. Rumour has it that as King lay dying he gave the constables the location of his Epping Forest hideaway.

On 4 May 1737, a gamekeeper named Thomas Morris, accompanied by a pedlar, tracked Turpin to Epping Forest. Turpin mistook them for poachers and said, 'There were no hares near that thicket'; to which Morris replied, 'No, but I have found a Turpin', and pulled his gun. Turpin spoke quietly to gain Morris's trust, then drew his own gun and shot Morris dead, before fleeing to Yorkshire with a £200 bounty on his head. The government issued a statement,

> *It having been represented to the King, that Richard Turpin did, on Wednesday, the 4th of May last, barbarously murder Thomas Morris, servant to Henry Thompson, one of the keepers of Epping Forest, and commit other notorious felonies and robberies, near London, his Majesty is pleased to promise his most gracious pardon to any of his accomplices, and a reward of*

Dick Turpin, the romantic highwayman.

£200 to any person or persons that shall discover him, so that he may be apprehended and convicted. Turpin was born at Thackstead, in Essex, is about thirty, by trade a butcher, about five feet nine inches high, very much marked with the small-pox, his cheek-bones broad, his face thinner towards the bottom; his visage short, pretty upright, and broad about the shoulders.

The following month the only contemporary account of Turpin as a highwayman was published, a broadsheet entitled *News news: great and wonderful news from London in an uproar or a hue and cry after the Great Turpin, with his escape into Ireland.*

In the summer of 1738, Dick Turpin earned money by stealing horses in Lincolnshire and returned with them to Brough to sell in Yorkshire. In July, he took a stolen horse to his father's home in Hempstead and swapped it for food and lodgings. It was a foolish move on both their parts because it landed John Turpin in Chelmsford prison for the winter on remand for receiving.

Dick fled north and bought a number of barns and stables just outside Corby. He assumed the name John Parmen and posed as a large-scale horse dealer. Outwardly, he became a wealthy and respectable member of the community. However, little were his customers aware that the horses he was selling were actually stolen from other owners in the two counties he was operating in (mostly acquired in Lincolnshire, as he was residing in Yorkshire). On occasion, he would even steal horses, wait a few months and then sell them back to their original owners. It was a risky business but one that for a time he got away with – and earned a lot of money into the bargain.

On 16 August, Dick Turpin stole three more horses. It was an act of stupidity two months later, on 2 October 1738, though, that got him sent to the gallows. He came home one night to his lodgings in the *Green Dragon Inn*, Welton, near Hull, about thirty-seven miles from York. He was drunk and, not having managed to steal anything, empty-handed. He shot a gamecock in the street belonging to John Robinson, his landlord, and when a neighbour, Mr Hall, said, 'You have done wrong in shooting your landlord's cock', Turpin threatened to shoot him as well.

When Mr Hall told John Robinson, they went to see a magistrate and Turpin was taken into custody. He carried no money and was unable to provide his own bail. As he was taken into custody at the house of correction at Beverley, Yorkshire, local authorities wondered how exactly 'Mr Parmen' made his money, and inevitably the constables learned of several outstanding complaints made against 'John Parmen' for sheep and horse stealing in Lincolnshire. He was taken to the dungeons of York's Debtors' Prison (now part of the York Castle Museum).

In February 1739, Turpin's identity was revealed when a letter from him was intercepted. He wrote to his brother-in-law who still lived in Hempstead:

> *Dear Brother,*
> *York, Feb. 6, 1739.*
> *I am sorry to acquaint you, that I am now under confinement in York Castle, for horse-stealing. If I could procure an evidence from London to give me a character, that would go a great way towards my being acquitted. I had not been long in this county before my being apprehended, so that it would pass off the readier. For Heaven's sake dear brother, do not neglect me; you will know what I mean, when I say,*
> *I am yours,*
> *JOHN PALMER*

However, these were the days before the penny post and his brother-in-law refused to pay the sixpence delivery charge. That sixpence cost Dick Turpin his life. The letter was returned to the post office which was run by John Smith (he was also the village schoolmaster, who had taught Turpin to read and write). Smith recognised the handwriting and travelled to York where he identified Parmen as Richard Turpin and earned himself a £200 reward.

On 22 March, Turpin was tried and convicted at the Grand Jury House in York of two indictments of horse rustling. When news of Turpin's arraignment leaked, crowds flocked to see him and it was said that his jailer made £100 selling booze to visitors. John Turpin's plea for transportation rather than death for his son was ignored. Dick spent the last of his money on new clothes and shoes and hired five mourners for ten shillings each. He gave hatbands and gloves to several other people and he also left a ring, and some other articles, to a married woman in Lincolnshire, with whom he had been acquainted.

On 7 April 1739, Turpin rode through the streets of York in an open cart, bowing to the crowds. Turpin was executed at Knavesmire (now the racecourse), York, on the Tadcaster Road. He had spent around thirty minutes chatting to the people and executioner. According to a local paper:

At the gallows he acknowledg'd himself to be the very man that shot the Keeper of Epping Forest; and also confess'd that he shot one of his comrades, for which he was very sorry, but shew'd no concern for shooting the Keeper, saying, it was no more than what he deserv'd.

The *York Courant* of 7 April 1739 reported:

With undaunted courage he looked about him, and after speaking a few words to the topsman, he threw himself off the ladder and expired in about five minutes.

The executioner was Thomas Hadfield, once Turpin's friend and a former Gregory Gang member who, as a condition of his pardon, agreed to be the hangman. The corpse was brought to the *Blue Boar*, in Castlegate, York, where it remained till the next morning, when it was interred in the churchyard of St George's parish. An inscription on the coffin gave the initials of his name, and his age. The day after the interment, body snatchers stole his body, but it was found in a garden belonging to one of the city's surgeons and reburied in the same place, this time with the addition of quicklime to destroy the remains rapidly. A headstone in the churchyard commemorates him, but is not at the precise location, which remains undiscovered.

And there the story of his short life would have rested had it not been for adventure books that began to appear at the start of the nineteenth century. It was here that the story of his fifteen hour, 150-mile ride on Black Bess to York to establish an alibi became public. Numerous inns along the A1 claim that Turpin stopped there for food or a drink or to briefly stable his horse. Historians have often claimed that Turpin never actually made the journey, and that the incident is pure fiction. The ride had been ascribed to the highwayman John Nevison, known as Swift Nick or Swift Nicks, a highwayman in the time of King Charles II who, to establish an alibi, rode from Gad's Hill (near Rochester, Kent) to York (some 190 miles) in about fifteen hours.

In 1834, the novelist Harrison Ainsworth used the tale of Dick Turpin's ride in his novel *Rookwood* and used dramatic licence to have Black Bess die at the end of the journey. Two years later, Martin Colnaghi published half a dozen high-quality prints outlining dramatic events from Turpin's career. These grabbed the public imagination and soon Dick Turpin became a staple of juvenile fiction, television programmes and films.

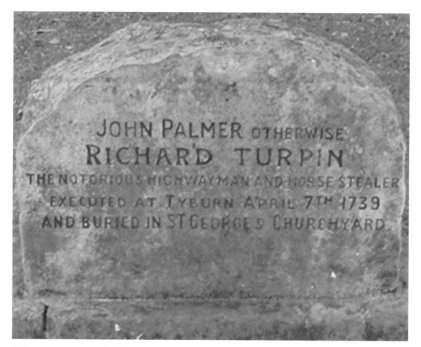

The gravestone of Dick Turpin where St George's churchyard once was. His body was dug up several times after his public execution in York in 1739.

Chapter 2

The Murder of Parish Constable Trigg

'Pratt fired again and shouted,
"Now damn your heart, I will do for you!"'

B erden is a small village on a back road between Newport and Bishops Stortford. It was there that Henry Trigg, the Parish Constable of Berden, was murdered.

Trigg, then thirty-six, was not a full-time policeman – parishes appointed a local man of good character to patrol the streets. In his every day life, Trigg worked as a cobbler. His shop was next to Berden Hall, in The Street, and he slept on the ground floor while his elderly parents stayed upstairs.

On the night of Friday, 25 March 1814, Thomas Turner and William Pratt visited Berden from Bishops Stortford. Turner had been to Berden before; he had bought a dog from a local called Chapman.

On his visit he noticed that Trigg had a large stock of leather in his shop and he told Pratt about his discovery. Together, the two men decided to rob the shop.

Pratt was described as 'a well looking man, with fair hair and good complexion, about 5 feet 10 inches in height', while his friend, Turner, was 'considerably shorter, a squat figure with a rather disagreeable obliquity of vision in his left eye'.

Just before midnight on that fateful Friday, Trigg heard a noise and went upstairs to warn his parents, saying he thought there might be thieves in the shop. Trigg and his father crept quietly down the stairs and, seeing two men, the younger Trigg set about Turner with his staff, encouraged by his father.

Pratt then attacked Trigg senior and a shot was fired, although it missed its target. The sudden appearance of the gun made the Triggs pull back and Turner got up, bloodied and beaten. Pratt fired again and shouted, 'Now damn your heart, I will do for you'. The bullet went straight into the younger Trigg's heart, killing him instantly.

Captured, both men attempted to blame the other. The duo appeared before Mr Justice Chambre at the Chelmsford Assizes and the jury quickly found them guilty. They were hanged along with two other murderers. Their corpses were used for medical research.

Chapter 3

William Calcraft
The First Private Hangman

'telling jokes on the scaffold,
playing to the crowd and drinking brandy!'

William Calcraft was Britain's longest serving executioner of all. He was also probably the most incompetent. He was noted for his 'short drops', causing most of his victims to be throttled rather than having their neck cleanly broken. On more than one occasion, he had to rush below the scaffold to yank on his victim's legs to finish them off.

It is not known precisely how many executions he carried out but it is estimated at between 400 and 450, including those of at least thirty-five women.

William Calcraft was born at Baddow, near Chelmsford in 1800. He earned his living as a shoe mender and once worked as a night watchman at Reid's brewery in what is now Clerkenwell.

Calcraft then landed a job selling pies around Newgate and became known to the execution staff and to the hangman, James Foxen, who dispatched his first victim in November 1824. Calcraft began to earn money working at Newgate, flogging juvenile offenders for ten shillings a week.

He was sent to Lincoln, where he presided over the executions of burglar Thomas Lister and highwayman George Winfield at Lincoln on 27 March 1829.

When Foxen died suddenly, aged 61, at his home in Booth Street, Hoxton, on 14 February 1829, Calcraft was appointed his successor and sworn in as London and Middlesex hangman on 4 April of that year. His first job was to execute the murderess, Esther Hibner, at Newgate nine days later. She had beaten and starved a ten-year-old girl to death. In prison Hibner tried to commit suicide and when she came to be hanged she was bound in a straitjacket. Such was the opprobrium in which

William Calcraft landed a job selling pies around Newgate prison.

she was held that when Calcraft appeared the crowd cheered him. During 1829 Calcraft dispatched thirty-one people. His pay for being the hangman was one guinea a week, with an extra guinea per capita for each execution and an allowance for cats-o'-nine-tails and birch rods.

Calcraft supplemented his earnings as London and Middlesex's official hangman by carrying out floggings at Newgate. He received one guinea a week retainer and a further guinea for each hanging at Newgate, and half a crown for a flogging. His earnings were greatly enhanced by executions at other prisons where he could charge higher fees, usually £10-£15. Calcraft was also the official hangman for Horsemonger Lane Jail in Surrey and received a similar recompense. Between April 1829 and October 1870, he hanged twenty-four men and two women there. He was the exclusive executioner at Maidstone prison, carrying out all thirty-seven hangings there between 1830 and 1872. As well as these not unsubstantial fees, he was also allowed to keep the personal effects and clothes of those he hanged, and he sold them to Madame Tussaud's for dressing the latest waxwork in the Chamber of Horrors. Added to this, if the victim had been infamous, Calcraft also sold the rope he had used to despatch them, selling it for one shilling per inch.

Calcraft claims to have invented the leather waist belt with wrist straps for pinioning the prisoner's arms, and one of the nooses he used (to execute Richard Pedder on 29 August 1857) is still on display at Lancaster Castle. It is a very short piece of 3/4" rope with a loop worked into one end, with the free end of the rope passed through it and terminating in a hook with which it was attached to the chain fixed to the gallows beam.

On New Year's Eve 1829, Calcraft carried out the last execution for forgery. Thomas Maynard and two accomplices attempted to defraud the Customs House by forging and cashing a warrant to the value of £1,973 (£134,000 at 2005 values). Maynard was hanged at the Old Bailey. Between 1830 and 1832 the House of Commons voted to abolish the death penalty for forgery but the House of Lords overturned each vote, although nobody actually suffered the ultimate penalty in that time.

Calcraft hanged those he was told to hang. In 1831 in Chelmsford he hanged a nine-year-old boy who had been found guilty of arson.

On 5 December 1831, before a crowd of 30,000, Calcraft hanged the body snatchers John Bishop and Thomas Head (aka Thomas Williams) at the Old Bailey. Bishop had been stealing bodies for a dozen years and was wont to boast that he had 'resurrected' 1,000 corpses. He admired the Edinburgh body snatchers Burke and Hare and was inspired when he learned that they had began murdering rather than just digging up dead bodies. How many people died at the hands of Bishop and Head is unknown, but we do know their last three victims: Fanny Pigburn, a boy named Cunningham and fourteen-year-old Italian, Carlo Ferrari.

Ferrari had an act with white mice that earned him an irregular living. One day, Bishop and Head, and another body snatcher, John May, lured him home and gave him rum and laudanum. When he was unconscious they tied his legs together and lowered him down a well and left him there until he drowned. They pulled out his teeth and sold them to a dentist and sold his body to King's College Guy's Hospital for nine guineas. The staff at the hospital became suspicious and detained Bishop and Head until the police could arrive. All three men were condemned and then Bishop and Head confessed that they had committed the murder. John May was reprieved because of the confessions but died shortly after. When it came to the executions Bishop expired at once but, thanks to Calcraft's usual incompetence, Head took some time to die and performed the 'Paddington Frisk' dance, caused by the involuntary body spasms (also known as the 'Tyburn Jig'). Appropriately, the bodies of both men were taken to anatomists – Bishop to King's College Guy's Hospital and Head to St Bart's.

Also at the Old Bailey on 9 January 1832, Calcraft hanged thirty-eight-year-old Eliza Ross, another body snatcher, for the murder of her lodger Catherine Walsh in Goodman's Yard, Whitechapel. Ross, who also went by the names Cook (after her common-law husband) and Reardon, was a frightful old soak. One day Mrs Walsh's daughter, Anne, came to visit and Ross told her that her mother had got up and left but she had no idea where she had gone. Anne Walsh fearing for her mother's safety began to trawl the streets looking for her. Eventually, she became suspicious and went to the police. When some clothes that had belonged to Catherine Walsh turned up, sold by Ross in a market, she and her eleven-year-old son, Ned, were taken in for questioning. Ross vehemently denied all knowledge of the elderly lodger. Ned was a different story. He revealed that he had seen his mother suffocating the old lady and putting her corpse in a sack. Despite a thorough search of hospitals and anatomists no body was ever uncovered but the testimony of young Ned was enough to send his mother to the gallows. As Calcraft put the noose around her neck she continued to protest her innocence and swore at all those who had 'betrayed' her, including her son. Like Bishop and Head, the body of Eliza Ross was dissected by medical schools of the Royal College of Surgeons.

On 2 May 1837, Calcraft hanged James Greenacre at Newgate. Greenacre had killed and dismembered Hannah Brown, 50, and parcelled her body around south London. Greenacre was well known around Westminster and his execution aroused great public interest. When he stepped out on to the scaffold, the crowd booed and Greenacre said to Calcraft, 'Don't leave me long with that pack of ghouls'. Oddly, the pie sellers did a roaring trade, the crowd associating the meat in the pies with the body parts of Hannah Brown.

On 20 April 1849 Calcraft hanged seventeen-year-old Sarah Thomas in Bristol. She had murdered her mistress after being cruelly treated. The mistress starved the girl and beat her. One night Sarah crept into her mistress's room and smashed her head in. Sentenced to death, she screamed as she was taken to the gallows, 'I won't be hanged! I won't be hanged…take me home'. As soon as she was over the trapdoor, Calcraft pulled the lever. He was to say later:

> *I never felt so much compunction in having to bring that young girl to the scaffold… She was in my opinion, one of the prettiest and most intellectual girls I have met with.*

The next day Calcraft was at Norwich Castle to hang James Blomfield Rush, a widower with nine children, who had murdered the Recorder of Norwich, Isaac Jermy and his son, Jermy, and wounded Jermy's daughter-in-law and maidservant, Eliza Chesney. On 28 November 1848, Rush, clad in a cloak, a red and black mask and a long-haired wig moved silently through the fog to Stanfield Hall, the home of Jermy. Unfortunately, Jermy heard something and went to investigate. As he opened the door Rush shot him dead. Jermy Jermy, too, went to investigate and was also shot and killed. Rush burst into the house firing as he went and riffled through whatever he laid his hands on. He shot both Mrs Jermy and Eliza Chesney before making good his escape into the fog.

Rush lived with his pregnant girlfriend, Emily Sandford, at Potash Farm. He had previously lived in Stanfield Hall Farm but had been evicted by Isaac Jermy because of bad debts and general incompetence at his job.

Rush was not the prime suspect. He was the only suspect. He said that he was with his girlfriend on the night of the murders and he produced a document supposedly written by Isaac Jermy absolving him of all his debts. However, despite his disguise, he had been recognised at Stanfield Hall and the police quickly established that the document was a clumsy forgery. Added to this evidence, Emily Sandford said that he was not with her on the night of 28 November.

When he came to trial in the Shire Hall, Rush conducted his

own defence. Never has the old adage in criminal trials that describes a person who represents himself at trial – 'He has a fool for a client' – been more apposite. Rush bluntly denied all the accusations, swore at the judge and tried to intimidate the witnesses. After a trial lasting six days, the jury retired for just six minutes – mostly taken up filing in and out of the jury room – before deciding a guilty verdict.

Calcraft hanged Rush shortly after midday before a huge crowd who cheered when the double killer went to meet his maker.

Later that year on 13 November, Calcraft hanged the husband and wife murderers Marie and Frederick Manning, both thirty, on the roof of Horsemonger Lane jail. Three years earlier, Maria De Roux, as she then was, became the lover of Patrick O'Connor, who was twice her age. O'Connor, a customs officer and money lender, had accumulated a fortune of £8,000 (£501,511 in 2004 values) but Maria also became involved with Frederick George Manning, a burly thug who had been sacked from his job as a guard on the Great Western Railway after being implicated in a £4,000 robbery. They married in 1847. Despite her marriage, Maria continued to sleep with Patrick O'Connor. It could not continue. On 8 August 1849, she invited him round for tea, but when he went to wash his hands in the kitchen she shot him in the back of the head. The bullet did not kill him and so Frederick Manning finished the job with a crowbar. They pushed the body into a hole they had dug in the kitchen floor and covered it with quicklime.

O'Connor's workmates reported him missing but when the police questioned the Mannings, they said they knew nothing of his disappearance. When the police returned three days later for further questioning, the Mannings had disappeared.

Both were apprehended, she in Edinburgh and he in the Channel Islands. When arrested each blamed the other for the murder and refused to speak to each other.

When they were found guilty, Frederick Manning received the death sentence quietly but his wife began shouting and tried to leave the dock.

The couple was hanged before a crowd said to number

50,000. Among them was Charles Dickens who wrote two letters to *The Times* decrying public executions and 'the wickedness and levity of the immense crowd', and suggesting that future executions be held in private. (It is thought that the character of Hortense in *Bleak House* was based on Maria Manning.) Dickens also complained about Calcraft. He said the hangman should refrain from telling jokes on the scaffold, playing to the crowd and drinking brandy!

A contemporary newspaper announces the execution of the Manchester Martyrs.

An even bigger crowd, estimated at around 100,000, watched Dr Edward William Pritchard being hanged in Jail Square near Hutcheson Bridge in Glasgow on 28 July 1865 for the murders of his wife, Mary Jane Taylor, and his mother-in-law.

Catherine Wilson was a serial poisoner whom Calcraft executed in front of the Debtor's Door at Newgate on 20 October 1862, witnessed by a crowd estimated at 20,000. She maintained her innocence to the end. Hers was the last public execution of a woman at Newgate.

In the 1850s (some sources say 1869), Calcraft's mother Sarah was a pauper in a workhouse at Hatfield Peveril, near Chelmsford, and Calcraft was told to help her. He declined, saying that his brother and sister should also help and, anyway, he had three children of his own to support.*

Calcraft became nervous, understandably so, when he was asked to hang Fenians and he received a number of death threats from disgruntled Irishmen. Nevertheless, on 23

---

* Calcraft was almost certainly wrong to say the burden should be placed on his brother, Charles. On 20 May 1840, Charles Calcraft was sacked from his job with the Little Baddow police force for visiting a prostitute while on duty. He had been a policeman for just nineteen days when he was sacked. It was all the more remarkable that he was allowed to join the force at all. He was sworn in shortly after being released from Colchester jail.

November 1867, Calcraft hanged three Fenians, William
O'Meara Allen, Michael Larkin and Michael O'Brien (alias
Gould), who had murdered a policeman in Manchester. They
became known as the Manchester Martyrs and a monument
was erected to them in Ireland.

In 1868 Calcraft officiated at the last public and the first
private executions. At Maidstone, on 2 April, he dispatched
Frances Kidder, the last woman publicly hanged, for the death
by drowning of her twelve-year-old stepdaughter, Louisa
Kidder-Staple. Eight weeks later on 26 May 1868, he hanged
the Fenian terrorist and stevedore Michael Barrett, who was
responsible for a bomb outside Clerkenwell prison that killed
twelve and injured more than a hundred.

An act of parliament restricting executions to private
locations was passed on 29 May 1868.

The first 'inside' hanging – that of eighteen-year-old Thomas
Wells – took place on 13 August 1868. Wells, who worked on the
railways, had, on 1 May 1868, murdered Edward Adolphus
Walshe, the stationmaster at Dover Priory railway station.
Calcraft used his 'short drop' and the attending crowd of
journalists and spectators were treated to the site of Wells taking
three to four minutes to die by slow strangulation.

Calcraft's last official act was the hanging of James Godwin
on 25 May 1874. He was, protesting, forced to retire, and
received a City of London pension of one guinea a week. Having
once been a genial man who took pleasure in breeding rabbits,
by the age of seventy he was described as surly and sinister-
looking, with long hair and beard, in scruffy black attire and a
fob chain. He wore a tall hat and walked with a slouching gait.
He died at Poole Street, Hoxton, on 13 December 1879.

After one execution Calcraft was asked what he thought it
must be like to be hanged. He replied:

*Well, I have heard it said that when you are tied up, and the trap
falls, you see the stones expanding and contracting violently, and
a similar expansion and contraction seems to take place inside
your own head and the breast. Then there is a rush of fire and
an earthquake, your eyeballs spring out of their sockets, and you
tumble down a precipice.*

Chapter 4

The Death of a Burglar

'The coroner allowed the Essex Constabulary to leave the body unburied. It was placed in the belfry of Strethall Church, where Nehemiah charged daytrippers three pence to look at it.'

On 28 February 1849 at 1 am, Nehemiah Perry was woken from his slumbers. He and his brother, Thomas, had retired at 10 pm the previous night when their housekeeper had gone home. The three of them lived in Strethall Hall, between Royston and Saffron Walden. The house is near Junction 9 of the M11. At Catmore End, around four fields away, lived Nehemiah's ex-wife, a gypsy. Her family believed that Perry looked down on them because they were gypsies and had made threats against Perry. His horses had been poisoned and so the brothers took loaded guns to bed with them each night.

Nehemiah Perry called to his brother and the two men, armed, crept to the top of the stairs. As they peered down into the darkness they saw a figure carrying a lantern with a mask over his face. He looked up and spotted the Perrys and called out for his friends to bring guns. Nehemiah Perry believed that this constituted a threat to his well-being and fired on the burglar. The two brothers fell to the floor and stayed prone for four hours until it became light and the housekeeper turned up for work. They heard but did not see the body being dragged away and saw no one else come into their house.

They slowly searched the house and found the burglar, a gunshot wound in his chest. They called the police and PC55 William Miller arrived at Strethall Hall. Soon the whole village arrived to gawp at the brothers and the corpse which was propped against a wall by Superintendent John Clarke.

Local opinion had it that Perry was merely defending his property and, if anything, deserved a medal. The local paper reported:

Various officers and others have seen the body of the dead man; indeed, hundreds of persons have visited the place; but no one has been able to identify him, although some assert that he has been in the neighbourhood during the past year with a nut-stall and target. His countenance is of a very forbidding kind and his head bears a general resemblance to that of Daniel Good, who was [hanged] for murder some time ago in London. Some silver and several false keys were found in his pocket. He appears to be about thirty years of age; 5ft 4in in height; sallow complexion, dark hair, the whiskers appear to have been worn large, but have recently been very closely trimmed and left very narrow; he appears to have been quite clean shaved within a short time of his death. His right eye tooth is out. He had on a white shirt, black and white neckerchief, one white cotton stocking, blucher boots tied in three holes, cord trousers, drab cloth double-breasted waistcoat, stout blue cloth coat with pockets inside, black Paris hat, apparently bought at Peterborough; a large pair of worsted stockings were drawn over his shoes, and this plan seems to have been adopted by the whole of the gang.

The identity of the dead man was unknown and so the coroner allowed the Essex Constabulary to leave the body unburied. It was placed in the belfry of Strethall Church, where Nehemiah charged daytrippers three pence to look at it.

After a time Benjamin Taylor, the Chief Constable of Peterborough, identified the corpse. It belonged to Abraham Green, alias Woods alias 'Little Abel', a ne'er-do-well known to the authorities throughout East Anglia.

Green's corpse was sent for dissection by George Paget at Cambridge. Three death masks had been made – one is in Saffron Walden Museum, another in Cambridge and the third was placed on a farmhouse where it remains to this day. Green's shattered breastbone was for a time on display to the anatomy classes for medical students at Cambridge.

Chapter 5

Was Queen Victoria's Surgeon Jack the Ripper?

'unanswered questions still remain.'

We do not know how many times the unobtrusive man set out with murder on his mind. Perhaps dozens. We do know that on four occasions between the end of August and second week in November 1888 he fulfilled his bloody aims.

Five women died at the hands of Jack the Ripper in London's East End. Five 'unfortunates', Victorian slang for a prostitute, aged between twenty-five and forty-eight, met grisly ends when they encountered the man regarded as the world's first serial killer.

But who was Jack the Ripper? Nearly 120 years after he last struck, the world is still awash with theories as to his identity. He was either a cricketer (Montague John Druitt), a prince (Albert Victor, Duke of Clarence), a cotton merchant (James Maybrick), a Jewish slaughterman (unnamed), a confidence trickster (Michael Ostrog), a former lover (Joseph Barnett), a directory compiler (Thomas Cutbush), a hairdresser (Aaron Kosminksi), a surgeon (Sir William Withey Gull), a known killer (James Kelly), a plumber (Frederick Deeming), a poisoner (Dr Thomas Neill Cream), a cobbler (John Pizer aka 'Leather Apron'), a painter (Walter Sickert), another surgeon (Vassily Konovalov), a quack doctor (Francis Tumblety), a philanthropist (Dr Thomas Barnardo), a shopkeeper (Edward Buchan), a military historian (Sir George Arthur), another doctor ('Dr Stanley'), Cambridge University fellow (James Kenneth Stephen), a journalist and sacked doctor (Robert Donston Stephenson), an insurance salesman (G. Wentworth

Bell Smith), a coroner (Dr William Wynn Westcott), a butcher (Jacobs), a sawdust seller (William Henry Bury), another doctor (Dr Cohn), yet another doctor (Frederick Chapman), still another doctor (John Hewitt), a former soldier (William Grant Grainger), a vagrant (Alfred Gray), a traveller (Frank Edwards), a barber (Severin Klosowski aka George Chapman), another surgeon (Oswald Puckeridge), a hairdresser (Charles Ludwig), a landlord (John McCarthy) and even a woman (Olga Tchkersoff).

The literature on Jack is voluminous and in 1976 one book was published that claimed that the Ripper was not one man, but three. Stephen Knight, a journalist on the *East London Advertiser*, a local newspaper, was sent to interview Joseph Sickert, the son of the painter Walter Sickert.

Knight came away with an incredible story that became a best-selling book. In his version Albert Victor, Duke of Clarence, known to his intimates as Eddy, had impregnated Annie Elizabeth Crook who worked in a tobacconist at 22 Cleveland Street, London W1 and lived in the basement of number six. Not only did he impregnate her but Albert Victor also married her, in secret. She gave birth to a daughter, Alice Margaret Crook, in the Marylebone workhouse on 18 April 1885. A young Irish girl called Mary Kelly who was a witness to the marriage was hired by Walter Sickert to be the child's nanny and moved into number six.

The affair became known to the establishment and in April 1888 the prime minister, Lord Salisbury, arranged for a raid on Cleveland Street. Eddy was taken back to Court and Annie Crook was sectioned at Guy's. She was to die thirty-two years later, on 23 February 1920, hopelessly insane, at 367 Fulham Road, London. Walter Sickert died at George's Hill House, Bathampton, Wiltshire, after a succession of strokes on 22 January 1942, and Alice Crook passed away in 1950. 'Their' son, Joseph William, was born on 22 October 1925. Mary Kelly, the nanny, told four of her friends about the affair between the prince and the shop girl. Salisbury, according to Sickert, could not allow this information to gain currency and so he ordered that Kelly and her friends be silenced forever.

Three men were entrusted with the task: – one, John Netley (born in Kensington, London, 19 May 1860; died at Clarence Gate, Regents Park, London, 20 September 1903 under the wheels of his own carriage), was to drive the carriage that transported the killer around London; the second was Physician in Ordinary to Queen Victoria, Sir William Gull; and the third was Walter Sickert himself, who acted as a lookout.

That was Joseph Sickert's tale. It was also, in many respects, utter nonsense.

There is no firm evidence to support the suggestion that Walter Sickert had children. His three recognised marriages were without issue. Alice Crook was indeed the mother of Joseph Sickert, but his real name was Joseph Gorman and his father was William Gorman. At St Aloysius's Chapel in St Pancras, on 14 July 1918, William Gorman married Alice Crook and their son, Joseph William, was born, as we have seen, in 1925. Suggestions that Gorman was impotent and Walter Sickert fathered his son, Joseph, seem far off the mark since Joseph had four siblings. All fathered by Sickert or did Alice put herself about a bit? Anyway, in 1978 Joseph confessed that his story was a hoax. He died in January 2003. Stephen Knight, who knew much of his book was nonsense and chose to suppress it, became a follower of the discredited Bhagwan Shree Rajnesh and changed his name to Swami Puja Debal. He died aged thirty-four of a brain tumour on 25 July 1985, while staying with friends at Carradale, Argyllshire.

Number six Cleveland Street was demolished in 1886, so a raid could not have occurred in April 1888 to spirit Eddy away from his wife and child. Annie Crook's whereabouts for 1888 are known, so she was not incarcerated against her will. In any case, it would have been impossible for Sir William Gull to wield the knife that killed the five prostitutes because he suffered a stroke in the autumn of 1887 that left him incapacitated.

So, there is no mystery about Sir William Gull? He was merely a doctor at the royal court. Not quite.

Sir William Withey Gull was born on New Year's Eve 1816 on board the *Dove*, a barge owned by his father, John Gull (1778–1827), a wharfinger of Thorpe-le-Soken. The *Dove* was at the time of the birth moored at St Osyth Mill, St Leonard, Colchester. He was the eighth of ten children of John Gull and his wife, Elizabeth Cooper, who came from Capel St Mary in Suffolk. Gull was baptised in Colchester on 9 February 1817. John Gull died of cholera in 1827 in London.

Ten years later, Gull became a medical apprentice at Guy's. The following year he matriculated at London University, and was offered free entry to Guy's medical school. Gull studied hard and won numerous prizes. In 1841 he graduated MB from London University with honours in physiology, comparative anatomy, medicine, and surgery, and became medical tutor at Guy's.

In 1843 he was appointed medical superintendent of the ward for lunatics, where he made many changes. That same year he became lecturer on natural philosophy at Guy's, a position he held for four years. For ten years from 1846 he lectured on physiology and comparative anatomy.

On 18 April 1848 he married Susan Anne Lacey in Guernsey and they had several children. From 1871 to 1883 and from 1886 until 1887 Gull served on the General Medical Council. In 1871 he became famous when he nursed the Prince of Wales through a bout of typhoid. In January 1872 Gull became Sir William and the next month was created a baronet.

Gull who bore more than a passing resemblance to Napoleon was in favour of vivisection and published papers on *anorexia nervosa*. His 'imperious, often sarcastic manner, and dogmatism alienated many colleagues'.

On 10 October 1887 while on holiday in Scotland he was felled by a stroke that left him paralysed. Another stroke, on 29 January 1890, killed him at his home, 74 Brook Street, Grosvenor Square, London, W1. He left £344,022 19s. 7d.

On 3 February Gull's body was transported from Liverpool Street to Thorpe-le-Soken where he was laid to rest. Many sent wreaths, including the Prince and Princess of Wales. Sir William Cameron Gull (1860–1922) succeeded him as second baronet.

But was Sir William Gull actually buried in Thorpe-le-Soken on that day? Many think not. One theory has it that another man was buried in the grave while Gull was sent under an assumed name to a lunatic asylum. Perhaps the coffin contained stones rather than any body at all.

Interviewed in the 1970s the verger of the churchyard commented, 'This is a large grave, about twelve feet by nine, too large for two people. Some people say that there are more than two buried there'.

Locals believe that Sir William Gull was not interred in February 1890.

The press reported the Whitechapel murders in gory detail.

Another mystery concerns Gull's will, which was probated in March 1890 and then again in 1897. Is this when Queen Victoria's physician in ordinary really died, after spending seven years in a madhouse?

And why was Gull's death certificate signed by his son-in-law, Dr Theodore Dyke Acland? Although it is not – and was not – illegal, it was certainly unethical behaviour since other doctors were present who could have signed the document.

On 28 April 1895 an American newspaper the *Chicago Sunday Times-Herald* ran a story about the mystic Robert James Lees (born at Hinckley, Leicestershire, 12 August 1849; died at Leicester, 11 January 1931), who claimed to have been taken to the London home of an eminent doctor who was later sectioned in an asylum under the name of Thomas Mason.

Was this Sir William Gull? Was there some reason that Gull's grave is big enough for three? Was he committed to an asylum? Why did his son-in-law sign his death certificate?

We can be sure that Sir William Withey Gull was not involved in the Jack the Ripper murders but unanswered questions still remain about this most eminent of Victorian physicians.

Chapter 6

The Slaying of Sergeant Eves

'Eves' body had been mutilated and his throat cut from ear to ear.'

Adam John Eves was born in Hutton and became a wheelwright. When he was twenty, Eves joined Essex County Constabulary. Life for police in Essex in those days was hard. Their beat was a large area, they had no meal breaks and were expected to work seven days a week – days off were not introduced until 1910. Violence against policemen was a regular occupational hazard.

Wages were poor – a constable 3rd class, such as Eves when he joined, received a salary of only twenty-one shillings per week. Discipline was harsh and the chief constable had the final say on punishment for policemen thought to have broken the rules. He could demote, fine or sack men he perceived to be miscreants.

In March 1877, Eves became Constable No 63. The following year he married Elizabeth and they moved to a cottage at Purleigh. Eves saw service throughout the borough before being promoted to the rank of Acting Sergeant and posted to Purleigh in January 1891. He was a good copper and as a result made some enemies among the criminal fraternity.

The evening of Saturday, 15 April 1893 started out normally for Sergeant Eves – he began his patrol and at about 10 pm popped into the *Royal Oak* pub. He chatted with the landlord and passed on a poster offering a reward for any information leading to the conviction of whoever was poisoning rooks in the area.

By midnight he had not returned home but since he often worked late, his wife was not worried and went to bed. She had

Sergeant Eves was murdered on duty. Essex Police Museum

heard a story about a local fire and assumed that her husband had been called to it.

The next day arrived but her husband did not. At 2.30 pm the local carpenter, Herbert Patten, walked past her cottage with his girlfriend and Mrs Eves asked if he knew anything about her husband's whereabouts. He did not and neither did he know anything about a fire. Elizabeth Eves replied, 'You never know whether they're going to be brought home dead or alive'.

Patten and his girlfriend carried on their way and came to the fields surrounding Hazeleigh Hall Farm, about a mile from Purleigh. As they crossed the grass they came to a spot known locally as Bellrope Gate. There they spotted that the ground was blood-soaked.

Peering into a ditch they saw the body of Adam Eves lying in the bottom in six inches of water. Eves' body had been mutilated and his throat cut from ear to ear.

Patten ran to Stow Manes where PC Chaplin lived and informed him of the gruesome find. As they returned to the site, they met Inspector Pryke who was making enquiries into the theft of corn from a barn at Hazeleigh Hall Farm. The two policemen examined the corpse and noted that his truncheon was still in his pocket and the shutter on his bulls-eye lamp was in the off position.

Under the body were three hefty sticks, one was broken in three but all were soaked in blood. The police discovered a bloodstained shovel and three corn sacks lying nearby. They followed a trail of spilt corn to Bell Rope Gate and noticed that wheel tracks led to nearby cottages.

As Eves' body was taken to his home, Superintendent Halsey sent a telegram to the Chief Constable with news of the murder and Captain Showers sent two of his men, Inspector Terry and Detective Sergeant Dale, to Purleigh to help with the inquiries.

The inquiry set up an HQ in the *Bell Inn*. The police learned of threats made against Sergeant Eves and quickly suspected a local gang of hooligans, one of whom, John Davis, thirty-four, had attacked Eves in July 1891 after he arrested him for poaching. Davis had been sentenced to two months' hard labour in prison.

As Pryke delved deeper into the case he noticed that false entries had been made in the farm ledger and a greater quantity of corn had been stored in the barn than was shown. Edward Fitch, the owner of the farm, estimated that thirteen bushels of corn were missing.

On Monday, 17 April, Inspector Terry and Sergeant Dale went to the house of John Davis but no one was there. Their next port of call was to his brother Richard Davis, a thirty-year-old labourer, where they discovered a handcart splashed with blood. PC Chaplin searched Richard Davis' garden and found three sacks of corn in the pond. Both men were arrested. Their associates, Charles Sales, a forty-seven-year-old dealer and John Bateman, thirty-seven, were both taken into custody that day. All four men had previous convictions for theft and poaching. They had all worked threshing corn at Hazeleigh Hall Farm.

During their interviews, Sales claimed that the blood on his waistcoat came from a bone he had bought. John Davis said that the blood on his cart was from a sheep's head that he had bought in Maldon on the day of the murder. The police also found blood on the back of Richard Davis's coat and shoes and on Bateman's clothes. All four were remanded to Chelmsford Prison for a week.

On Wednesday, 19 April, Thomas Choat made a statement to police claiming that he had heard James Ramsey, the driver of the threshing machine at Hazeleigh Hall Farm, make threats against Adam Eves.

The Monday after the murder Ramsey had turned up for work wearing new clothes. James Ramsey and his son John, the chaff boy, were arrested and taken to Maldon Police Station. When their home was searched police discovered a pair of trousers soaked in blood. Choat told the police that James Ramsey had been wearing them on the day of the murder. The Ramseys were also remanded in custody.

On 24 May 1893, John and Richard Davis, Charles Sales and

James Ramsey were committed for trial at the Essex Assizes. There was little evidence against John Bateman and John Ramsey and they were released without charge.

The trial began at Chelmsford Assizes on 3 August 1893 before Mr Justice Mathew. Prosecuting was Mr Crump QC. All four defendants pleaded not guilty to the murder of Sergeant Eves. Opening for the prosecution Mr Crump said that Sergeant Eves had stumbled across the men as they stole corn from Hazeleigh Hall Farm. When he challenged them, they murdered him and threw his body into the ditch where it lay undiscovered until Herbert Patten took his girlfriend for a walk.

Mr Crump produced evidence that a cart belonging to Richard Davis had left wheel tracks where Eves had been murdered. Davis said that he had used the cart to collect stones from that field. A spade found in the field also belonged to him.

On 4 August 1893, Charles Sales was freed after the prosecution produced no evidence. The three remaining defendants continued to protest their innocence claiming that they were asleep at the time of the killing. They said that any of the other men who worked on the farm could have committed the crime and that all the evidence against them was circumstantial.

The judge did not seem to agree and in his summation told the jury that the theft was pre-planned and that the thieves were also responsible for the murder of the policeman.

The jury retired at 3.26 pm and returned at 4.46 pm. Their verdict for the Davis brothers was guilty, but they acquitted James Ramsey. The judge donned the black cap and passed the death sentence.

Richard Davis lodged an appeal against his conviction but for brother John it was too much and he confessed to the murder. He revealed that the three men had been in the commission of robbery when they were disturbed by Sergeant Eves. As he attempted to stop them, he and John Davis fell to the ground and James Ramsey struck the policemen on the head with his cudgel. As Eves lay dazed on the ground, Ramsey slit his throat.

Richard Davis had not been involved in the murder. The confession saved Richard Davis's life and his death sentence was commuted to life imprisonment.

John Davis was hanged at Springfield prison, Chelmsford on 16 August 1893.

The funeral of Sergeant Eves took place at Purleigh Church a week after his murder. The Chief Constable led the cortege and more than 150 members of the police force attended. Grieving villagers lined the route to the church. Mrs Eves was given a pension of £15 per year, and a public subscription raised £400.

Chapter 7

The Randy Book-keeper

'She had been shot from so close that
the wound was blackened with gunpowder.'

James Canham Read was a handsome, thirty-seven-year-old book-keeper. Despite his rather boring job, he was charming and married with eight children, living in Stepney, east London. Read was paid £3 a week by the Royal Albert Docks at North Woolwich in south London where he had worked for twenty years.

A ladies' man, he also kept a string of girlfriends. One of his girlfriends was Louisa Bertha Ayris who lived at 24 Wesley Road in Southend-on-Sea. In September 1890, he met her younger sister, Florence Dennis. Read became infatuated with the young woman and began a simultaneous affair with her and another woman, Beatrice Kempton, who lived in Mitcham, Surrey. He was also still sleeping with his wife.

In October 1893, Beatrice fell pregnant. Read, who had brown eyes and stood 5ft 7in, could not commit bigamy so he persuaded her to live with him in a bed-sit in Rose Cottage in Mitcham. They rented the room as Mr and Mrs Edgar Benson. Their baby was born on 6 January 1894.

Read's pocket was being stretched by his colourful love life. He had one wife, one pretend wife and nine children to support. (He had also fathered a child by Mrs Ayris, born in May 1892, but did not support it.) Then, to add to his woes, Florence Dennis fell pregnant in 1894. Her mother arranged for Florence to stay in Southend with her sister.

Once settled in Southend, Florence wrote to Read asking him what arrangements he would be making for her. Read replied asking to meet to make provision for his tenth child. Florence

Victoria Station. James Read met Florence Ayris here. Paul Donnelley

set off to meet Read at Prittlewell on 24 June 1894. She was never seen alive again. Louisa Ayris sent a telegram to Read enquiring after her sister but Read wrote back:

Dear Mrs Ayris – What is the meaning of your extraordinary wire? Please write fully. I have not seen the young person for quite claimed 18 months, when you are at St John's Hill.

Back in London, Read stole £159 12/6 from his employer, intending to set up home permanently in Mitcham as Edgar

Benson with his 'darling Beatty'. Read made the fatal error of writing to his brother from Rose Cottage. He was arrested by Detective Inspector Baker of Scotland Yard after Florence Dennis's body was found by Frederick Rush, a local, in a watery ditch, with a gunshot wound to the head on the evening of Monday, 25 June 1894. She had been shot from so close that the wound was blackened with gunpowder.

Read was committed to Springfield Prison on 30 July and, after being remanded in custody six times, he was sent for trial on 7 September 1894.

The trial of 'The Southend Murderer' opened at the Shire Hall in Chelmsford Assizes on 12 November 1894 before Mr Baron Pollock. He was the last judge to bear the title Baron of the Court of Exchequer. The case for the prosecution was led by Frank Lockwood, QC, MP, the newly appointed Solicitor General. Read was defended, perhaps appropriately, given his womanising ways by Mr Cock, QC.

More than 300 people applied for tickets for the public gallery. Read pleaded not guilty to the charge of murder but before the murder trial had begun pleaded guilty to theft from the Royal Albert Docks.

The Solicitor-General rose to his feet and outlined the case:

So far back as August 1889, the prisoner made the acquaintance [on the pier at Southend] of Mrs Ayris, the wife of John Ayris [a milkman] and the eldest sister of Florence Dennis. That acquaintance ripened into an intimacy, and there is no doubt that immoral relations existed between the prisoner and Mrs Ayris. In December 1889, Mrs Ayris [moved from Clapham Junction] to 189 St John's Hill Road, Wandsworth. The prisoner was then corresponding with her, but not under her own name or at the address where she was living with her husband — this for obvious reasons. He was writing under an assumed name. He addressed her as Mrs Neville, and his letters were sent to 137 St John's Hill Road, a stationer's shop. We find the prisoner and Mrs Ayris spending a day at Leigh in the spring of 1891... We subsequently find they were staying at Buckingham together. The immoral relations between Mrs Ayris and this man ceased about March 1892. There was another meeting in March 1894, at Victoria Station, when she told him it was her intention to take a lodging-house at Southend, and asked him to recommend lodgers.

In September 1890, on one occasion when Mrs Ayris and the prisoner were out walking [on Clapham Common], they met Florence Dennis, I suggest by chance. Mrs Ayris introduced Florence Dennis [and another married sister, Emma Deed, who was with her], and they passed on... Florence [who was eighteen] was then living part of her time with her mother, but throughout the case you find she has resided alternately with her mother [at Sheerness in Kent] and Mrs Ayris. In May 1892, a child was born — I think it was Mrs Ayris's second child. Florence Dennis went to her sister's. There was a nurse there, a Mrs Schmidt, and she will tell you that during that time...she posted two letters for Florence Dennis, at her request, and both the letters were addressed to Mr Read, at the Albert Docks. One night Florence was absent from her sister's house, and she remained out until late.

In 1893 we find Mrs Ayris living at Hanwell, and Florence Dennis at Sheerness, and Florence Dennis corresponding with Read, addressing letters from and receiving them at 63 High Street, Sheerness, where a woman of the name of Hughes was manager. Evelina Dennis, a younger sister of the murdered woman, fetched the letters for Florence, and these letters were addressed to 'Talbott'. Some of the documents we have are in disguised writing by the prisoner. One of the visits paid by Florence Dennis to Mrs Ayris at Hanwell was in October 1893, and when the body of this unfortunate woman was examined, it was found to contain a child that must have been begotten about that time. After Christmas 1893, letters to the name of Talbott were addressed to the Post Office, Sheerness... The correspondence ceased in May 1894, and Florence Dennis was murdered in June 1894.

I take you now, gentlemen, to another scene, and introduce you to another name. In 1892 the prisoner made the acquaintance of a young woman named Kempton, who was living in Gloucester Road, at a [confectioner's] shop. The prisoner met her at [Gloucester Road] railway station, and introduced himself as a Mr Edgar Benson, of 16 North Street, Poplar. He described himself as a traveller on behalf of Messrs Peck, tea merchants, of Cheapside. Correspondence took place, and meetings took place, and according to the sad story Miss Kempton will tell you, she was seduced by the prisoner in the spring of 1893. Miss Kempton had a home at Cambridge, but she left there to go to Hallingbury, where she lived under the care of the prisoner. The prisoner explained his absence from her there by stating that his business kept him away. But he was able to spend from Saturday to Monday with her. On 6 January 1894, a child was born to Miss Kempton by the prisoner. In February, Miss Kempton moved into lodgings provided for her by the prisoner at Rose Cottage, Mitcham.

The prisoner has a brother, named Harry Read. The name by which he was introduced to Miss Kempton was 'Mr Edwards', a friend. 'Benson' told Miss Kempton that he himself had a sister at Canterbury, married to a man named [Walter] Parker. Harry Read – 'Edwards' as he was known to Miss Kempton – lived at 16 North Street, Poplar. But he was dismissed from there...

In April 1894, Miss Kempton notices that the prisoner is exhibiting considerable anxiety, and he tells her it is his pecuniary position that troubles him. But, gentlemen, what was it really? Florence Dennis conceived her child in October 1893, and by this time, April 1894, no doubt her condition must have been made known to herself, and to the prisoner.

I told you the prisoner spent from Saturday to Monday, as a rule, with Miss Kempton. From Christmas 1893 to the day of the murder, June 1894, he never spent one Sunday at his own house, where his own wife and family lived, at Jamaica Street, Stepney. With three exceptions he spent a portion of the Saturdays, and a portion of the Sundays, during 1894, with Miss Kempton at Rose Cottage, Mitcham. Gentlemen, these three dates are 20 May, 10 June, and 24 June. He wrote to Miss Kempton to excuse himself for his absence on the first date, and stated that he had gone to Canterbury, on most important business on behalf of Walter [Parker] whose child was ill with bronchitis. Gentlemen, there was no such child ill, and what he said was false. Florence Dennis at this time was living in Sheerness [Kent]. On Saturday, 19 May, she went out at night and did not return home until about 10.30. I now come to the next date, 10 June. On 8 June he writes to Miss Kempton: 'I am making arrangements to go to Canterbury tomorrow, Saturday, on important business, so let me beg of you to do your best to keep up your spirits until I come back. I do not expect I shall be back before Monday.' On 22 June, this is the excuse the prisoner gives for not going down to Miss Kempton: 'I am sure you fully share with me my regret that I shall not be with you this weekend. I have to go to Canterbury on most important business of Walter's. He has asked me to do this, and I cannot refuse. If I can utilise this opportunity to lift myself out of my present critical condition I will do so. But if I do not succeed in this, God knows what I shall do. I'm dead broke.' Absolutely untrue! There was no business at Canterbury — he did not go to Canterbury – he had no relations at Canterbury. I shall be able, I think, to show you — that he was at Southend — that he was at Prittlewell.

I will now resume the story of Florence Dennis. In June 1894 she was eight months advanced in pregnancy. A communication was made to her mother, with whom she was living at Sheerness, and on 19 June she was removed to Mrs Ayris's house at Southend. On Friday, 22 June, the prisoner wrote to Miss Kempton to say that he was going on Saturday to Canterbury on most important business. That Friday he was loitering away his time with his brother and a friend named Kendall [they met at 10.05 pm]. Another telegram is dispatched to Florence Dennis. I am prepared to show that the telegram is in the handwriting of the man who was in company with the prisoner at the time – I mean Harry Read. Harry Read it was who sent that telegram from a Post Office near Charing Cross [at 9.25 pm]. That telegram was received by Florence Dennis on [Saturday] 23 June. You will hear that Florence Dennis went out...

All these telegrams were dispatched in a curious way. Instead of being handed over the counter, they were put into the post, so as to give no opportunity of the sender being identified. The prisoner carried about with him, it seems, telegraph forms and stamps.

I come now to the Sunday, 24 June, the day on which the murder was committed. Florence remained about [her sister's] house until the evening of that day, and an arrangement had been made by her, with her sister's knowledge, that owing to the crowded state of her sister's house, she should pass the night in a room taken for her at an adjoining house.

On that evening she went out to meet somebody – and by any of her relations she was never seen alive again.

That Sunday afternoon, a lady named Mrs Kirby met the prisoner in a wheatfield, coming from Prittlewell. The prisoner asked the way to Leigh. She said she didn't know, and he said: 'Oh, I may as well go back to Rayleigh again.' And he turned back. He was not seen again by anyone we are in a position to call until a little after ten, when a man named Robert Dowthwaite, coming from Prittlewell, meets a man and a woman, whom he identifies as the prisoner and – having seen the dead body – the murdered woman, walking arm in arm along an avenue towards the field in which the murder was committed. Another witness, Richard Golding, who with his family had been in a public house at Prittlewell, came along this same road, and he saw a man coming down the avenue alone – a man whom he afterwards identified as the prisoner.

The man who went up the avenue was with a woman – the man who returned was alone. But the prisoner is seen again, by a policeman named Daniel, at Benfleet, early the next morning [at 1.15 am]. The prisoner said he wanted the road to London.

Later we find him calling at the house of a fellow clerk at Leyton-stone, who was ill [at about 9.20 am]. When he called at the house his appearance was not as usual – he had not that smart, dapper appearance which he usually presented. He had no gloves in his hand, and presented a dishevelled appearance. At about ten o'clock [on the Monday] he arrived at his office at the docks, a little later than usual. But that was explained by his call at the fellow clerk's. At 12.30 he went out and got shaved. Later, a clerk named Burgess went into the prisoner's room at the office, and found him burning a fire. He asked what it was for, and the prisoner made some remark about foul air. At 3 pm, a telegram is received [at the office] by him from Mrs Ayris. The telegram was one inquiring: 'Where is Florrie?' The answer was a letter saying that he had not seen Florence Dennis for 18 months.

On Monday, 25 June Mrs Ayris goes round to the house where her sister had been staying the previous day. She is startled to find that Florence Dennis is not there. She waits. After waiting some time she gives information to the police, and then telegraphs to the prisoner, asking where Florence was. The body at that time had not been discovered. Mrs Ayris did not know that her sister was murdered... When [the prisoner] got that telegram from Mrs Ayris he knew perfectly well that the hue and cry had commenced. He knew that Mrs Ayris knew his address in Jamaica Street, and that there he would probably meet an officer to arrest him. He knew that to stay at the Royal Albert Docks was to court apprehension but there was one place Mrs Ayris did not know, a place known only to his brother Harry – viz, Rose Cottage, Mitcham. Therefore you are not surprised to hear he leaves his work earlier than usual, without signing off [and] takes with him a bag, which probably contained the money, to stealing which he has pleaded guilty. Why was he fleeing? Because, I say, he was the only man who knew of that murder. He goes to the address known practically only to himself and his brother, in whom he has confidence. And at 4.30 he dispatches the following letter-card to his brother: 'My dear Harry – Secure my desk contents and report everything to me at M—. In strict secrecy. Will explain when I see you. Allay all fears. JCR'.

Well then – between eight and nine o'clock on the Monday night the prisoner arrives at Rose Cottage, Mitcham. He is dressed in a black coat and vest, grey trousers, a light brown hat, and a light coloured tie. He has money with him, and he accounts for that by saying he has borrowed it from Mr Parker. There is some alteration in his whiskers – he has them cut more closely to his face – and this is the commencement of a disguise which he afterwards developed. Miss Kempton remarks on his appearing tired and weary. He accounts for it by saying that he has been to Canterbury. That is untrue.

On 26 June the prisoner went to Croydon, where he bought a ready-made [light grey] suit, the clothes, I think, in which he now sits in the dock. From that time he no longer wears the clothes he was wearing on 25 June. He leaves off shaving, and when Miss Kempton asks him why, his first reason was that he had no razor with him. When Miss Kempton suggested that he should go out to be shaved, he said it was too much trouble. He stays indoors much more than usual. On 27 or 28 June he is absent from Rose Cottage, and Miss Kempton receives a telegram from him, asking if all is right. On 30 June she receives another telegram asking her to wire if all is well. What was the cause of his anxiety? His anxiety was to ascertain if any person was on his track – if so, he would not return.

In July, Inspector Baker and Sergeant Marden go to Rose Cottage to apprehend the prisoner.

Now how was this young woman, Florence Dennis, killed? Beyond all doubt it was by a bullet wound. Gentlemen, the revolver is not forthcoming but the bullet is. Above the left ear there is a circular wound, about a quarter of an inch in diameter. The edges of the wound are blackened and singed, showing that the revolver must have been held very near to the head of that woman, and the conical bullet was found embedded in her brain. What was the weapon used? You may remember in the opening part of my speech, I alluded to an address: 16 North Road, Poplar. That was the place from which Harry Read was discharged at Christmas 1892, for some misconduct. Some time before that Harry Read purchased a revolver. He, at this time, got very low in spirits, and on one occasion threatened to take his own life. The prisoner, who was present at the time, expostulated with him, calling him a fool, and took the revolver away. Mrs Kelly, a sister, took the cartridges away.

In January 1894 this revolver was seen in the house of the prisoner at Jamaica Street, and was afterwards seen also by Miss Kempton, while they were at Hallingbury. In April 1894 the prisoner's daughter [Emma Read] will tell you she saw at the house in Jamaica Street a revolver case in the sitting-room – and the prisoner had a pocket made to carry it... I can show the bullet was a 7-Eley, was in a pin cartridge, and was of conical shape. This woman's death was caused by a bullet which would fit exactly the cartridges which were used in this revolver, which is traced to the prisoner's possession, and is seen in the prisoner's possession until April 1894, and which has not been seen since.

Mr Lockwood sat down at 1.40 pm and the court adjourned for a thirty-minute lunch. When the court resumed Mr Lockwood called several witnesses to back up the prosecution's case. The day finished with Evelina Read stating that she had seen her dead sister posting letters to Read.

The next day Emma Dennis, the dead girl's mother, testified at her upset when she learned that her unmarried daughter was pregnant by a married man.

The next witness was Mrs Ayris who was ashamed of the fact that she had been exposed as an adulteress and that she had shared a lover with her sister. Her answers were mainly monosyllabic. She agreed that her affair with Read had begun in September 1889, two years after her marriage. The affair continued until March 1892, two months before she gave birth to Read's child. Beatrice Kempton also gave evidence against her lover.

On the third day Harry Read took his turn in the witness box. He was by turns evasive and provocative.

The final witness for the prosecution was Detective Inspector Baker. A statement made by Read was read out to the court in which he claimed that he was innocent. No witnesses were called for the defence and after lunch Mr Cock began his closing statement. He finished saying, 'No fact proved before you is sufficient to bring home any guilt to this man'. The court adjourned at 4.30 pm.

The fourth and final day opened with the Solicitor General making his closing statement. He sat down at 11.25 am and Mr Baron Pollock gave his direction to the jury. He spoke for eighty minutes, finishing at 12.50 pm, after which the jury retired. Forty minutes later, they had reached a verdict. The foreman, G Thorpe Bartram, announced 'Guilty' when the clerk of the court asked if they all agreed on a decision.

Read again protested his innocence before Mr Baron Pollock donned the black cap to pronounce sentence of death.

At 7.45 am on Tuesday, 4 December 1894 the funeral bell

began to toll at Springfield Prison in Chelmsford. James Canham Read was given some brandy and he asked if death by hanging was instantaneous. At 7.55 am the fog that had covered the prison began to lift. By 8.03 am when the black flag was unfurled, executioner James Billington had done his job. Read was buried within the confines of the prison.

Chapter 8

The Moat House Farm Murder

*'a small boot was discovered and
inside it a skeletal foot'*

Samuel Herbert Dougal was born in Bow, east London in May 1846 and began working as an apprentice in a civil engineering office. Dougal had received only a basic education but he wanted to better himself and, anyway, life as an apprentice was far too boring for him. A bearded, burly cockney, for some reason he spoke with an Irish accent. On 6 March 1886, he joined the Royal Engineers at Chatham and stayed with the regiment for twenty-one years. He served in Ireland, Wales and ten years in Nova Scotia, Canada. He worked as a surveyor and clerk. He took full advantage of the Queen's uniform and developed a reputation as a ladies' man. He fathered a number of illegitimate children around the world.

Ladies' man and murderer, Samuel Dougal. Chelmsford Museum

In 1869, he settled down and got married or, rather, he got married. It was a stormy marriage and his wife, Lovenia Martha Griffiths, bore him four children. He drank and, according to some sources, beat her. The marriage lasted until June 1885 when Mrs Dougal suddenly became ill and twelve hours later died, aged thirty-seven, in Halifax, Nova Scotia.

Dougal was sent home on compassionate leave but when he returned in August 1885, he had a new wealthy wife, Mary Herberta Boyd. In early October 1885 she was also taken ill with severe vomiting and died. She was just twenty-eight years old. Both wives were buried within twenty-four hours of their deaths. Since both had occurred on a military base, there was no requirement to be noted in a civil register.

In 1887, the regiment sailed for home to celebrate Queen Victoria's Golden Jubilee. Dougal was accompanied by a young Nova Scotian girl whom he passed off as his wife. He fathered a child by her but Dougal was so brutal that she returned to Halifax and claimed that she was a widow.

When he left the Army, Dougal flitted from job to job. He was a salesman, shopkeeper, surveyor, clerk and publican. He also flitted from woman to woman. A widow bore him two more children but he regularly beat her up and, eventually, she walked out on him. He was for a time a publican in Ware, Hertfordshire, running the pub with an elderly woman and her money. However, during his tenancy, both the pub and the house attached to it burned down. Dougal had insured them both and when he tried to make a claim, he was arrested for fraud. He was tried at St Albans in December 1889 but acquitted through lack of evidence. On his acquittal he moved to Ireland where he met Sarah White and on 7 August 1892, in Dublin, Dougal married for the third time.

In 1894 he returned to London without his wife and began looking around for another meal ticket. One day as she left a Camberwell bank, Emily Booty met Samuel Dougal. He charmed her and soon persuaded her to lease and furnish a house for them in Watlington, Oxfordshire. Then the third Mrs Dougal travelled over from Ireland with the offspring and moved into Miss Booty's house. The poor woman put up with this for several months during which time the younger child died of convulsions.

Eventually, it all became too much for her and she began to pack. Dougal became agitated by this and threatened her so she left without any of her possessions. She did not go quietly, however, and went to the police. They came to the house and searched Dougal's possessions and found some of Miss Booty's smaller goods in them: a linen-duster, two table cloths and four yards of dimity. He was arrested and charged but when the case came to court in April 1895 at Oxford Quarter Sessions, Dougal defended himself and was so impressive that the jury found him not guilty.

Seven months later, he was not so lucky. In January 1896, he appeared at the Central Criminal Court charged with forging the signature of Lord Frankfort on a cheque whilst he was working in the office of the Commander of the Forces in Dublin. Found guilty, he was sentenced to one year's hard labour. After being sent to Pentonville he began to suffer from acute depression and two months into his sentence he made an attempt to hang himself in his cell. He served the rest of the sentence in Cane Hill Lunatic Asylum.

In December 1896, he was declared sane and released. He was in dire straits having lost his Army pension when he earned a criminal record. It was his brother, Henry Dougal, who saved him by offering him some clerical work in Biggin Hill. Sarah Dougal came back to him but left to return to Dublin with Olive, their surviving child, when Dougal's behaviour became intolerable. It became so bad that Henry sacked his brother and Dougal had no choice but to return to London.

In September 1898, he met Camille Cecile Holland, a fifty-five-year-old spinster who had been born in India after her French mother married a Liverpudlian. She was living at 37 Elgin Crescent in Bayswater, west London. The meeting happened either at the Earl's Court Exhibition or possibly through a lonely hearts advertisement. She was charming and educated but naïve. She dyed her hair red and wore too much make-up. She played the piano, wrote songs, painted and was a devout Roman Catholic, attending Mass regularly. She was still a virgin after an early boyfriend, a young naval officer, drowned. She was also wealthy – £6-7,000 (around £450,000 at today's values) – and if there was one thing Dougal liked as much as women it was money. He wooed her and told her that he was Captain Dougal. They even spent a weekend together in Southend at the Royal

Camille Holland was used and murdered by Samuel Dougal. Chelmsford Museum

Hotel. In November 1898, she told her dressmaker that she had realised Dougal only wanted her for her money and had broken off the relationship.

Dougal was not a man to give up easily. On 2 December, he rented a furnished house, Parkmoor, at Hassocks near Brighton for £6 per month. The rent was paid by Camille and on 5 December she left Bayswater to move in with 'Captain Dougal' in Brighton. It was highly unusual for a Victorian lady to move in with her boyfriend yet that is what she did. The couple spent Christmas and New Year together in Hassocks and it was probably then that Dougal began planning her death.

In January 1899, they bought Coldhams Farm in Quendon, near Clavering, for £1,550 and renamed it Moat House Farm. It was a remote building; the nearest house was the Rickling Vicarage, which was about half a mile away. The contract made between the estate agent named Dougal as the owner until Camille had second thoughts and had the farm registered in her name on 19 January.

On 26 January, the couple moved to 4 Market Row, Saffron Walden to be near their property and stayed there for three months while the farm was being readied for occupation.

Dougal spent much of his time in local pubs and probably was a regular visitor to the *Grapes* in Bishop's Stortford. The publican there was one George Chapman, who would be hanged for the murder of his three wives.

Dougal and Camille moved in on 27 April 1899. Two days later, Lydia Faithful, 20, arrived as their maid. She left a week later, probably disgusted at Dougal's leering.

On 9 May, nineteen-year-old Florence Havies was hired to replace Lydia. She began work on 13 May – she, too, lasted barely a week. Dougal made a pass at the servant. She was to say later:

[He] came down alone and into the scullery where I was. He came up unawares and kissed me. I objected very much, and as soon as I saw Miss Holland I made a complaint to her.

On 16 May, Dougal again made a pass at the serving girl, smashing his way into her bedroom. He claimed, 'I only wanted to wind up the clock in her room'. Camille was very upset by Dougal's behaviour and threatened to walk out, or throw him out. Dougal feared losing not her but her money.

She begged Florrie to stay on and the two women slept in the same bed on Wednesday 17 and Thursday 18 May to keep each other company.

On Friday 19 May, Dougal and Camille went for a drive in their trap, ostensibly to get some supplies from town – she was never seen alive again.

It was 8.30 pm when Dougal returned in the trap alone. He told Florrie that 'the mistress ha[d] gone to London'. The next day, when Camille had still not returned, Dougal told Florrie that he had received a letter from Camille and that she had gone on holiday. Florrie left the same day.

Dougal moved his wife and daughter into Moat House Farm. He told locals that she was his widowed daughter. Eventually, the pretence was dropped and it became known that she was the real Mrs Dougal. In turn, she told anyone who asked that Camille was away on a yachting expedition.

The trap in which Samuel Dougal probably murdered Camille Holland.
Chelmsford Museum

The police became suspicious over the length of the yachting holiday and began to take an interest in Samuel Dougal and Moat House Farm. He answered all their questions willingly but they were dissatisfied and began to investigate his finances.

He had begun to forge her signature on cheques and letters shortly after her disappearance. Piecemeal, he began to acquire her money and belongings and by September 1901 he had £2,912 15s (about £210,000 at current values) and also transferred ownership of Moat House Farm to himself. With his newly acquired wealth, Dougal was the first local to own a car and was seen in the grounds teaching naked girls to ride a bike.

In January 1902, Sarah Dougal left, annoyed at her husband's behaviour and ran off with an engine driver, George Killick. In May, Dougal sued for divorce and an uncontested decree nisi was issued on 1 August 1902.

In September, Kate Cranwell, another servant, went back home after Dougal impregnated her. He stupidly decided to contest the paternity suit. The baby was born in January 1903.

As the years went by, more and more people began to wonder where was Camille Holland. Most of her possessions were still at Moat House Farm and yet she had not been heard of for almost four years. The rumour mill went into overdrive.

The police sprang into action and Camille's nephews, bankers and solicitors were contacted. None had had word of her.

On 4 March 1903, Superintendent Pryke visited the farm and had a conversation about the rumours in the village. He said, 'I thought he had told me the truth and I shook hands with him on leaving'.

The walls were closing in on Samuel Dougal. On 5 March, he withdrew £605 from his accounts and travelled to London where he stayed at the Central Hotel in Long Lane. On 9 March the decree nisi was rescinded. On Friday, 13 March, he and Georgina Cranwell, a sister of Kate, who was pregnant by him, travelled to London with luggage that was left in the cloakroom of Liverpool Street Station. They then went to Bournemouth for the weekend. They returned to London on Tuesday, 17 March.

Samuel Dougal and Georgina Cranwell.
Chelmsford Museum

She then returned to Moat House Farm while he stayed in London.

The next day, Dougal went to the Bank of England at 1.30 pm and handed over fourteen £10 notes and asked that they be broken down into smaller denominations. The eagle-eyed cashier, William Lawrence, spotted that some of the notes had been stopped and asked Dougal to accompany him to Mr Dale, the secretary's office. He was asked to endorse one of the notes and wrote, 'Sydney Domville, Upper Terrace, Bournemouth'. Meanwhile, Detective Inspector Henry Cox was summoned and asked Dougal to go with him to the detectives' office in Old Jewry. As the two men went into the street, Dougal made a dash for freedom but, unluckily for him, he ran into Frederick's Place, a cul de sac. After a brief fight, Samuel Dougal was arrested for 'forging and uttering a cheque value £28 15s payable to J Heath, dated 28th August 1902, purporting to be drawn by Camille C Holland at Clavering'.

About his person he had eighty-three £5 notes, eight £10 notes, £63 in gold, a £5 gold coin, seven rings (five women's and one belonging to Camille), five watches, six moonstones, a walking stick, other items of female jewellery, a pipe and a cloakroom ticket.

On 19 March, police began to examine Moat House Farm. The *Essex County Chronicle* reported: 'The police officers engaged in the searching at the Farm occupy the farmhouse,

Police drained this moat in their search for Camille Holland. Chelmsford Museum

preparing their meals and making their beds for themselves. Detective-Sergeant Scott acts as chef.' For five weeks they searched the farm and the moat, then a further investigation revealed that around the time of Camille's disappearance Dougal had been seen filling in ditches. Excavation began on the ditches and on Monday 27 April – four years to the day since her arrival – a small boot was discovered and inside it a skeletal foot. The search continued and Camille's badly decomposing body was discovered – with a bullet in the head. The bullet had come from Dougal's service revolver. He had leaned over and shot her a few inches above and behind the right ear as she had

The remains of Camille Holland were kept in her greenhouse prior to forensic examination. Chelmsford Museum

her back to him. The body was identified by her small (size two) feet. The *Essex County Chronicle* described the scene near the farm when the body was discovered:

Throughout the week, people have flocked to the Moat House Farm in crowds, the majority of the visitors being ladies.

Oranges and nuts were sold as at a village fair, and the raucous voices of the vendors were heard on every side. Souvenir postcards of the Moat House and of the grounds, showing many of the holes made by the police and the tent-like awning which conceals the grave, commanded an enormous sale. A number of the sightseers brought Kodaks with them in search of effective snapshots and a still larger contingent were relic-hunters.

Three days later, on Thursday, 30 April, in the dining room of Moat House Farm, Detective Inspector Alfred Martin charged Samuel Dougal with the murder of Camille Holland. On Monday 22 June 1903, in Shire Hall, Chelmsford Assizes, it was indicted that Samuel Herbert Dougal, 'on the 19th May 1899, did feloniously, wilfully, and of his malice aforethought, kill and murder Camille Cecile Holland at Clavering'.

The trial opened before Mr Justice Wright at Chelmsford on 22 June 1903. Prosecuting was C F Gill, KC, and Dougal was represented by George Eliott. The next day, at 3.55 pm the jury retired and at 4.50 pm they returned a guilty verdict. The judge donned the black cap and said:

It is my duty to pass upon you the sentence of the law – that you be taken from hence to the place from whence you came, and from there to a place of execution, and that you there be hanged by the neck until you be dead, and that your body be afterwards buried within the precinct of the prison in which you shall have been last confined after your conviction. And may the Lord have mercy on your soul.

Dougal said nothing as sentence was passed.

After his appeal was dismissed, Dougal wrote to the Home Secretary and claimed that the gun had gone off accidentally. He added that he had placed her on some straw in the ditch but that when he got up the next morning the ditch was being filled.

At Springfield Prison, Chelmsford on the morning of his execution, 14 July 1903, he ate a breakfast of bread and butter, and a fried egg and drank some tea. He also took a few sips of brandy, given to him by the warders.

At 7.30 am Reverend J W Blakemore, the chaplain, entered the condemned cell and told Dougal to make peace with God. They spent a little time praying and the vicar later reported that Dougal seemed more composed.

Shortly before 8 am, the High Sheriff, Under Sheriff, prison governor, a doctor, the executioner William Billington and his assistant, John Ellis, walked in. Dougal was given a glass of brandy and water – which he downed in one – to steady his nerves. He spent a short time sorting out his personal effects and making his bed. At 7.58 am Billington strapped Dougal's hands behind his back and followed the High Sheriff, Under Sheriff and prison governor as they walked the few yards towards the death cell, a room about twelve feet square with whitewashed walls.

The trapdoor was placed in the floor and when Dougal noticed some chalk marks he went and stood on them. Billington moved swiftly and placed a leather strap around Dougal's legs, tightened the noose around his neck and placed a white cap over his face.

Just before Billington carried out the final act, the prison chaplain asked the condemned man to reveal or deny his guilt before God. Dougal was silent and the chaplain again shouted, 'Are you guilty or not guilty, Dougal?' The split second before the trap door opened, he was heard to mumble, 'Guilty'. Dougal fell 6ft 8in and disappeared into the pit. His body twisted violently for a short while before coming to a halt. Dougal was cut down and his corpse taken to the mortuary for an inquest.

He was buried in the grounds of Springfield prison and only his initials and a number on the wall mark his final resting place. Outside the jail, a crowd of small boys watched and waited.

At the inquest, the prison governor said that the execution was carried out efficiently and the prison doctor, Dr Newton, stated that death was instantaneous and the execution was carried out to his satisfaction. The jury agreed.

Chapter 9

The Honeypot Lane Murders

*'Two shots rang out in quick succession
at 5.30 am that day'*

T he first historical reference to Basildon is in records from 1086. It is mentioned in the Domesday Book as Belesduna. It was, until after the Second World War, a collection of sprawling farms that were mostly inaccessible. Basildon was designated as a new town after the war to accommodate people who wanted to move from London. Basildon was created from Pitsea, Laindon and Vange. Since 1974 Basildon has been a useful political barometer: the way Basildon goes, so goes the country.

Honeypot Lane is today home to a parade of council houses, situated off the A1321 (Broadmayne). In 1906, a journalist from the *Southend Telegraph* said that it was 'little more than a track, five miles from Billericay, five miles

from Pitsea, extending from the main road to the Laindon Road'.

Half a mile from Basildon Rectory was the home of the devoutly religious Albert and Emma Watson. He was forty-seven and she three years older. They kept themselves to themselves after their move from Kilburn. They lived off their land and animals, running a small poultry farm and market garden, although they had no running water. They got their water from a pond 300 yards away on the land belonging to their neighbour Richard Buckham, of Sawyers Farm. Mr Buckham did not take the same pride in his land as the Watsons did in theirs. By the summer of 1906 the pond had dehydrated and had only eighteen inches of water in it.

Richard Buckham left for work each morning at 6 am, walking to Laindon to catch the 6.45 am to London, leaving his wife, Margaret Ann, and two teenage sons, Richard, nineteen, and Robert Charles, sixteen, at home.

On Wednesday 23 August 1906, the teens took their father's guns and went out to shoot rabbits even though they had been warned by both parents not to touch the weapons. Two shots rang out in quick succession at 5.30 am that day, followed by another after a brief pause.

At 10 am that Wednesday the two boys ran to the main Billericay road where they bumped into Thomas F Stevens, a neighbour. They blurted out breathlessly that two people had drowned in the pond. Mr Stevens knocked on a few doors and a group went to the pond where they saw Albert Watson almost submerged in the pond and his wife's body lying nearby.

The local bobby, PC Samuel B Lazzell, was summoned and he oversaw the transfer of the bodies to the Watsons' cottage before calling Sergeant Richard Giggins of Billericay, an officer with more than twenty years service behind him. When he examined the bodies, Giggins found that Albert Watson had one large wound in his back, his wife had wounds on her neck, chest and arm and it appeared that she had been shot twice.

Richard Buckham came home from London and Robert told him that the Watsons had committed suicide. The next morning, the experienced Superintendent Alfred Marden arrived on the scene and questioned the Buckham boys. It was too much for Robert. He began crying and told the police that his brother had shot the Watsons. Both were charged with murder and bound over for trial.

They were tried at the Essex Assize in November 1906. Robert was acquitted. Ronald Walker, Richard's defence barrister, portrayed his client as mentally incompetent in a bid to avoid the gallows.

The prosecution case, led by J Harvey Murphy and D R Chalmers Hunt, claimed that the Buckham boys did not like their father giving away their water to the Watsons. An argument likely ensued and Richard settled it with extreme violence. The bodies had three wounds, which meant that Richard would have had to reload the gun and thus it could not have been an accident. After the murders, the brothers looted the Watsons' home and stole 4s 6d and a watch.

The jury retired to consider their verdict. The foreman of the jury, Harry Amos of Braintree, later recalled:

After the first hour's deliberation we were summoned back to the court by the bailiff. We were equally divided, six of our number considering the prisoner's mental condition was such that he could not be responsible for what he had done. I told the judge this, and after his plain advice, we retired again. The number of jurors who dissented from a verdict of willful murder was reduced to three. One of those in particular would not give in and wanted me to tell the judge the same thing again but I refused. It really looked as if we would be shut up for the night and I began to make preparations for the event. After further deliberation however, we all agreed.

Mr Justice Lawrence passed sentence of death on 10 November 1906. Richard Buckham, now aged twenty, was hanged at Springfield Prison by Henry Pierrepoint on Tuesday, 4 December 1906.

The Watsons were buried at Great Burstead Church.

Chapter 10

The Killer Toyboy
and the Housewife

'Yes, darling you are jealous of him...
be jealous so much that you will do something desperate'

I t was not until the 1980s that a vogue for toyboys – much younger male lovers of older women – became a recognised phenomenon. The pop star Sinitta even had a Top 10 hit record entitled *Toyboy* in 1987. Britt Ekland, the Swedish actress, was also celebrated for her love of toyboys.

However, if anyone thought that it was a new trend, they would be disabused of the notion when they read the story of Edith Thompson and Freddy Bywaters.

Our story begins on 11 June 1921. Percy Thompson, a thirty-one-year-old shipping clerk who worked in the City of London, went on a week's holiday to Shanklin on the Isle of Wight. With him were his twenty-seven-year-old wife, Edith, her twenty-five-year-old sister Avis, and Avis's boyfriend Freddy Bywaters, 19, and another couple.

Edith Jessie Graydon was born on Christmas Day, 1893 at 97 Norfolk Road, Dalston, east London, the eldest of five children of William Eustace Graydon (born at Dalston 1867, died February 1941), a clerk with the Imperial Tobacco Company, and his wife, Ethel Jessie Liles (born 17 December 1872, died at 231 Shakespeare Crescent, Manor Park, East Ham, London E12, January 1938), the daughter of a policeman, Alfred Cooper Liles. The other children were Avis Ethel (born 24 September 1895, died in King George Hospital, Ilford, 6 August 1977), and three younger brothers, Newenham E (born 1898), William (born 1900), and Harold, known as Towser (born 1902).

When Ethel was five, the family moved to 231 Shakespeare

Crescent in Manor Park, East Ham. Edith was a bright child who was good at maths and enjoyed acting and dancing. In 1911, her dexterity with numbers enabled her to land a bookkeeper's job at Carlton and Prior, a firm of milliners at 168 Aldersgate Street in the City of London, EC1, not far from Aldersgate tube station (now Barbican). She was a popular employee, quickly rose through the ranks to become chief buyer, and twice went to Paris on buying trips. According to her biographer, 'she was by now an attractive, auburn-haired young woman who stood 5ft 7½ in tall [and] read voraciously'. Some time in 1909, she met Percy Thompson (born 1890, died 1922) and they discovered they shared an interest in the theatre.

In 1914, as the hostilities were beginning in the bloodbath that would be the First World War, Edith Graydon and Percy Thompson holidayed in Ilfracombe, Devon. On 15 January 1916, they were married in St Barnabas's Church, Manor Park. A little while after, Percy Thompson joined the London Scottish regiment, but received an honourable discharge a few months later on medical grounds. By his own admission, he had conned the army medic into believing that he had a heart condition after smoking fifty cigarettes a day for a month.

This action changed Edith's feelings towards her husband. She believed that Percy was, if not a coward, then certainly guilty of cowardly behaviour. Her brother, Newenham, was serving in the same regiment, and a beau of her sister Avis would die at Passchendaele in 1917.

In April 1916, the Thompsons moved into rented accommodation at 25 Retreat Road, Westcliff and lived there until September 1919 when they moved to 65 Mansfield Road in Ilford.

In June 1920, they bought, for £250, 41 Kensington Gardens, a substantial house in Ilford with a spacious garden and moved in the following month. The previous owner was keen to sell because it had two sitting tenants. Fanny Lester and her ailing husband (who was to die on 14 May 1922) stayed on in the house as the Thompsons' lodgers paying 30 shillings a month.

Frederick Edward Francis Bywaters was born on 27 June

1902. He was raised in Manor Park although when his father died his mother moved to Upper Norwood in south London. Handsome and impulsive, he joined the Navy during the war by lying about his age and then the merchant navy and impressed friends and women with his tales of exotic, faraway places. By the time of his holiday with the Thompsons, he was a mess steward with the Peninsular and Oriental Steamship Company. In January 1920 he visited the Graydon family home in Shakespeare Crescent to see his old school friend, Edith's younger brother, Billie. There was an instant spark between

Edith and Percy Thompson made their home in this large house, 41 Kensington Gardens in Ilford. Paul Donnelley

Bywaters and Avis and they began to see each other. He also became a lodger at 231 Shakespeare Crescent.

And so to the holiday…

It was at Shanklin that Edith Thompson and Freddy Bywaters realised their mutual attraction. Their holiday companions were oblivious to what was developing between the couple. None more so than Percy Thompson. In fact, on 18 June at the end of the vacation he even invited Bywaters to leave Shakespeare Crescent and move into 41 Kensington Gardens, near the Ilford golf course, as their lodger.

On 27 June 1921, Freddy Bywaters and Edith Thompson had lunch in the Holborn Restaurant and later that day slept together for the first time – at least that is the official version.

However, extracts from the letters written by the couple were released by the Home Office on 1 January 1986 that prove that the affair began much earlier, possibly in the autumn of 1920.

On 1 August 1921, Percy and Edith Thompson had an argument and, as she related, he 'struck me several times and eventually threw me across the room'. Bywaters leapt to the defence of his lover and told Percy to divorce his wife, much to the annoyance of the cuckolded husband who ordered the younger man out of his home – Bywaters moved out four days later.

From 5 August, Bywaters stayed with his mother in Westow Road, Upper Norwood, London.

On 11 August, she wrote to him, 'Darlingest – Will you please take these letters back now? I have nowhere to keep them, except a small cash box I have just bought and I want that for my own letters only and I feel scared to death in case anybody else should read them…'. It is the first letter that was written that is still existent.

Nine days later, she wrote again, 'Come and see me Monday lunchtime, please darlint. He suspects'.

On 9 September 1921, Bywaters sailed for the Orient aboard the SS *Morea* and Edith began writing him passionate letters. Between 9 September 1921 and 23 September 1922, he made five voyages on the *Morea*: 9 September until 29 October 1921; from 11 November 1921 until 6 January 1922; 20 January to 16 March 1922; 31 March to 25 May 1922; and lastly from 9 June until 23 September 1922. Back on shore, the affair went on for twelve more months, during which Edith became pregnant twice.

During the affair Bywaters spent long spells away from his inamorata. She wrote him sixty increasingly passionate letters and told him she would do anything to be with him, even going so far as to kill her husband. He addressed letters to her at her office and then to a *poste-restante* addressed to Miss P Fisher at the Aldersgate post office. Only two of his letters to her are still extant. She lied to Bywaters telling him that she was mixing glass and poison in her husband's food. She wrote in one:

It must be remembered that digitalin is a cumulative poison, and that the same dose harmless if taken once, yet frequently repeated becomes deadly'. Darlingest boy, the above passage I've just come across in a book I am reading, Bella Donna *by Robert Hichens, Is it any use?*

At the subsequent trial two leading pathologists, including Sir Bernard Spilsbury, dismissed the claims that Percy Thompson had been given poison as patently false.

During the late summer of 1922, Bywaters tried to finish with his older lover, perhaps realising the affair had no future.

In another letter, written on 19 September, she wrote:

Darlingest boy – I don't quite understand you about 'Pals'. You say 'Can we be Pals only, Peidi, it will make it easier'. Do you mean for always? Because if you do, no, no a thousand times… Have you lost hope and given up hope? Yes, darling you are jealous of him – but I want you to be – he has the right by law to all that you have by right of nature and love – yes darlint, be jealous so much that you will do something desperate.

On Saturday, 23 September of that year, Bywaters was back in Britain and went straight to his mother's in Upper Norwood. However, his old passion with Mrs Thompson resurfaced. On Monday, 25 September, they met up – albeit only for an hour – at Fenchurch Street station after her work. They spent much of the following weekend together.

On the morning of Monday, 2 October, Edith rang Bywaters and they met for lunch and went to *Fuller's* tea room for supper after work. A letter – undated – was read at the trial. She had written:

Darlingest lover of mine, thank you, thank you, oh thank you a thousand times for Friday – it was lovely – its [sic] always lovely to go out with you. And then Saturday – yes I did feel happy… Darlint, we've always said we'll always be Pals, haven't we, shall we say we'll always be lovers… Or is it (this great big love) a thing we can't control… Your love to me is new, it is something different, it is my life… It seems like a great

welling up of love – of feeling… just as if I was in your hands…
its [sic] physical purely… Darlingest when you are rough, I go
dead – try not to be, please.

Darlint – do something tomorrow night will you? Something
to make you forget. I'll be hurt I know, but I want you to hurt
me – I do really – the bargain now seems so one-sided – so unfair
– but how can I alter it?

Did Edith give Bywaters the letter on the Monday night and, if
so, was the line 'do something tomorrow night will you' an
incitement to murder? Had Thompson and Bywaters planned
Percy Thompson's murder the weekend they saw each other?

At 9 am on Tuesday, 3 October 1922 Edith rang Bywaters and
they met for lunch at the *Queen Anne* restaurant in Cheapside.
When they finished their meal, Edith went back to Carlton and
Prior. At 5.10 pm they met at *Fuller's* and stayed for 15 minutes
before he walked her back to Aldersgate station. He left and her
husband met her. It is possible that Bywaters watched the husband
and wife walk away. Bywaters went to see the Graydons in
Shakespeare Crescent and stayed for four hours, leaving at 11 pm.

Meanwhile, back in the West End the Thompsons and Lily
and John Laxton, her aunt and uncle, went to the *Criterion*
Theatre at 222 Piccadilly to see Cyril Maude in Ben Travers' new
farce *The Dippers*. They got the Tube and then the 11.30 pm
train back from Liverpool Street and alighted at Ilford. They cut
down York Road and on to the very long and badly lit Belgrave
Road. They walked on the right hand side of the pavement. It
was after midnight on 4 October and they were not far from
their home when Freddy Bywaters leapt out on them at the
junction of Belgrave Road and Endsleigh Gardens, having
hidden in the garden of number 59.

He pushed Edith to the ground and shouted at Percy
Thompson, 'Why don't you get a divorce or a separation, you cad?'

Thompson replied, 'I know that's what you want. But I'm not
going to give it to you. It would make it too pleasant for both of
you'.

With the adrenaline flowing, Bywaters stabbed Percy

Freddy Bywaters hid in the front garden of this house as he waited to ambush Percy Thompson. Paul Donnelley

Thompson four times with a six-inch double-edged sheath knife. One cut sliced Thompson's carotid artery and he died drowning in his own blood a few minutes later. Edith was heard to cry, 'Oh don't, oh don't', loudly enough to be heard two streets away. Bywaters ran away and fled through Seymour Gardens where he threw the knife down a drain. He arrived home around 3 am.

A doctor on the scene somehow misdiagnosed the stabbings and said that Percy Thompson had haemorrhaged. Edith told the police that her husband had been walking along Belgrave Road with her and suddenly started bleeding from the mouth.

At Ilford police station on the afternoon of the next day, she revealed that she had recognised her attacker, dressed in a grey trilby and a dark raincoat and named Freddy Bywaters. Believing herself to be a witness and not an accomplice, she told the police about the affair and a cache of sixty love letters. The police took a different view and on 5 October both Thompson and Bywaters were arrested and were jointly charged with the

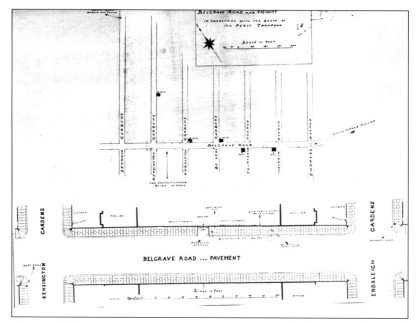

A map of the area.

murder of Percy Thompson, she with being a principal in the second degree. The police believed that she had been the guiding light behind the crime, guiding her young lover.

The trial opened in Court No 1 at the Old Bailey on 6 December 1922. The indictments against Edith Thompson were murder, conspiracy to murder, attempting to murder and inciting Freddy Bywaters to murder her husband but she was only charged on the first count. It created a public sensation and seats were said to be changing hands for £5 each. The jury consisted of eleven men and one woman. Bywaters was defended by Cecil Whitely, KC, and was a model defendant – model from the police and prosecution's point of view. He showed them where he had stashed the murder weapon and told them that his lover did not know what he was intending to do. He said that he had only intended to confront Percy Thompson but he lost his temper when Percy took a superior attitude and struck out.

Thompson was defended by Sir Henry Curtis-Bennett, KC, who opined that she was a bored housewife who longed for some excitement. It was a strategy that appeared to be working until she insisted on going into the witness box, probably in the hope of saving Bywaters and possibly because she enjoyed being a celebrity.

Edith Thompson was not an impressive witness. She was, in turn, coquettish, melodramatic and self-pitying. She also contradicted herself on several points.

Sir Henry said:

She spoiled her chances by her evidence and demeanour. I had a perfect answer to everything, which I am sure would have won her an acquittal if she had not been a witness. She was a vain woman and an obstinate one. Also her imagination was highly developed, but it failed to show the mistake she was making… In short, Mrs Thompson was hanged for immorality.

Edited extracts of the love letters were read out in court. Forty-nine letters, notes and telegrams were produced as exhibits, thirty-four were not – including those covering her periods (or lack of them), her two pregnancies (resulting in one abortion in January 1922 and one miscarriage or possibly another abortion in late June 1922) and a sexual congress *al fresco* in Wanstead Park.

Sir Thomas Inskip, KC, (later Lord Caldecote), the Solicitor General, who was aided by Travers Humphreys, lied to the jury when he said that Edith Thompson's correspondence contained the 'undoubted evidence' of a 'preconcerted meeting between Mrs Thompson and Bywaters at the place' – i.e. the murder scene. The letters did not contain that evidence, but the jury could not know this.

He told them:

All you are asked to consider is whether Mrs Thompson incited Bywaters to kill her husband, and the letters are important from that point of view. They are important to show that she so worked and preyed on the mind of this young man by her suggestions that, although it was his hand that struck the blow, it was her mind that conceived the crime.

The killing zone – Bywaters stabbed Thompson. Paul Donnelley

The press called her the 'Messalina of Ilford' and the judge, Sir Montague Shearman, told the jury, 'You should not forget you are trying a vulgar and common crime', and his summing up was to say the least prejudicial. He said:

This charge really is – I am not saying whether it is proved – a common or ordinary charge of a wife and an adulterer murdering the husband... You are told this is a case of great love. Take one of the letters as a test – 'He has the right by law to all that you have by right of nature and love'. If that means anything, it means that the love of a husband for his wife is something improper... and that the love of a woman for her lover, illicit and clandestine, is something great and noble. I am certain that you, like any right-minded person, will be filled with disgust at such a notion.

It was partly this attitude that led some to believe that Edith Thompson was on trial for adultery as much as, if not more than, for murder.

On 11 December after two hours of deliberation, both were found guilty and Mr Justice Shearman donned the black cap to pass sentence of death on them. Thompson became hysterical and started screaming in court, while Bywaters loudly protested his lover's innocence.

On Boxing Day, as she waited in prison for her fate to be decided, Thompson wrote a letter to her friend Bessie Aitken:

Dear Bessie,

I wanted to write to you yesterday and yet I couldn't. I could do nothing but sit and think. Who was it said, 'Some days we sits and thinks, and some we simply sits'? Well, yesterday was a 'sitting and thinking day'.

I got your little letter on Saturday. Yes, the result of the appeal was a great shock – I had such hopes of it – not only hopes for mercy, but hopes for justice; but I realise how very difficult it is to fight prejudice.

If you have facts to fight, and you fail, you seem more reconciled, but when it's only prejudice – oh, it's awful.

You talk about not having to suffer the extreme penalty. Do you know that I don't dread that at all. I feel that would be far easier than banishment – wrongful banishment for life. I feel no apprehension of what might lie ahead after this life.

Yesterday I was twenty-nine; it's not really very old, I suppose, and yet it seems so to me.

I suppose when you're happy age doesn't count; it doesn't seem to matter; it's when you're not that the years seem so frightening.

Yesterday I was thinking about everything that has ever happened, it seems to help in all sorts of ways when I do this. I realise what a mysterious thing life is. We all imagine we can mould our own lives – we seldom can, they are moulded for us – just by the laws and rules and conventions of this world, and if we break any of these, we only have to look forward to a formidable and unattractive wilderness.

I've often thought how good it would be to talk, to pour out everything, it might have pained as well, but it would be pain that comes with sudden relief of intolerable hurt.

However, I'm going to forget all that now. I'm going to hope

– because everybody tells me so. I'm going to live in those enormous moments when the whole of life seems bound up in the absolute necessity to win.

Thank you so much for writing to me, and helping to keep me cheerful.

EDITH

A petition was started against the death sentences and 832,104 people appended their name to it.

Ethel Graydon wrote to the Queen while Avis appealed to Andrew Bonar Law, known as the 'Unknown Prime Minister', for clemency.

Avis wrote:

> *231, Shakespeare Crescent*
> *Manor Park*
> *E12*
> *30/12/22*

Sir

Re my sister Mrs Thompson

I beg you kindly to read this letter in the hope that some of the points will enable you to see my sister's character other than presented to the public, by the prosecution.

I can assure you Sir that my sister had no idea that her husband was going to be murdered, as it had been arranged a fortnight before that, I should accompany them to the Theatre, & spend the night with her in Kensington Gdns, & she had no idea until she met her husband in the evening that I was not going to be of the party. Her husband telephoned me late in the afternoon & I told him that I had already made arrangements to go out for mother. How can they pass sentence of Death on her?

Dr Spilsbury gave evidence that there was no trace of poison in the deceased's body, how then can it be said she poisoned him. Why was all the evidence of defence put on one side, & only the black side – the foolish letters of an overwrought, unhappy woman – placed before the Jury.

It is untrue that my sister was happy until Bywaters came into her life.

Mrs Lester can prove, & also others with whom she lived before, that she was unhappy; only her great respect & love for her parents, prevented her bringing her troubles home. If she had done anything wrong any time, she would have told mother at any cost, also my brother-in-law, would have spoken to my dad.

I should like to say, that Percy Thompson being of a peculiar character had no friends of his own, & naturally very soon disagreed with my sister's friends.

The man is dead, but why should he die blameless? His case was just the same as my sister's which you can see by the letters, not produced.

Mrs Thompson was a hard working woman, of a generous, loving nature & no doubt after Bywaters seeing her unhappiness, she turned to him for sympathy. Her great mistake – being afraid to confide in her family who loved her above everything. Why was it so emphatically said 'She incited Bywaters'? It is obvious her letters are answers to questions, where are Bywaters letters to prove his statement that Mrs Thompson is innocent? Why has no benefit of the doubt been given in this case to the accused!

Can it be my sister is insane! Is this question having the prison doctors' attention?

If you had seen my sister at any time, there could not be any doubt in your mind that the verdict is wrong.

I beg you to show mercy on her, for her parents sake, you are a father therefore understand their feelings.

We are helpless & know she is Not Guilty.

May the Great Judge of all guide you in coming to your final decision, to which the family are just clinging, as the last hope.

Committing the above to your kind attention.

I remain in anticipation

AVIS E. GRAYDON (Miss)

To

The Rt. Hon. Bonar Law Esq. M.P

It was to no avail. The home secretary, William Bridgeman,

dismissed an appeal and the death sentence was scheduled for am on 9 January 1923.

As that day drew near Thompson became hysterical and refused to eat. On the morning of her death she was heavily sedated before being hanged at Holloway prison by John Ellis, assisted by Robert Baxter and Thomas Phillips, becoming the first woman to be executed since 1907. She was half-carried to the scaffold and had to be held upright for the noose to be placed around her neck.

Oddly, she had also gained a stone between the death sentence and the execution. Freddy Bywaters was taken to Pentonville where he occupied the same cell as Dr Crippen and Frederick Seddon. He was dispatched by William Willis, assisted by Seth Mills, at the prison. Both Thompson and Bywaters were buried within the prison grounds where they had died.

It was later revealed that as she dropped 6 feet 10 inches through the scaffold Edith Thompson suffered a large haemorrhage, leading to speculation that she may have been pregnant at the time. All women hanged after Thompson wore canvas knickers to prevent a recurrence of the massive bleeding suffered by Thompson.

In the 1950s and 1980s a campaign was started to clear Edith Thompson's name. At 10.15 pm on 31 March 1971, her body was reinterred in plot 117 of Brookwood Cemetery in Surrey and her grave was consecrated on Saturday, 13 November 1993 by the Reverend Barry Arscott of St Barnabas's, the church in which she had been married almost eighty years earlier.

As she was awaiting execution in the death cell, Edith Thompson's mother berated her for the sexual content of her correspondence with Bywaters. 'How could you write such letters?'

She replied, 'You never saw the letters he was writing to me!'

Chapter 11

Who Killed PC Gutteridge?

'As he lay on the floor he was
shot in each eye.'

It is a horror story familiar to students of true crime. On 27 September 1927, Police Constable Gutteridge was on patrol on the Ongar-Romford road when he stopped a stolen car driven by two petty crooks: Frederick Browne, 47, and William Henry Kennedy, 36. The driver pulled out a pistol and shot PC Gutteridge and then, believing an old superstition that the eyes capture the last image seen before death, unloaded an extra bullet into each eye of the stricken policeman. Four months later, Browne was arrested at his Clapham garage accused of stealing a car. He became linked to the Gutteridge murder when a Webley revolver was found on his premises. Kennedy was arrested in Liverpool and confessed to being with Browne on the day of the shooting but claimed that Browne had pulled the trigger. Ballistics played an important role in the case and both men were charged with the murder of PC Gutteridge. They were both hanged in May 1928. And that was that as far as most were concerned, but was it the truth of what really happened on that chilly autumn day 80 years ago?

Dr Edward Richardson Lovell, a local GP, returned home at 7.30 pm on Monday, 26 September 1927 and parked his blue Morris Cowley (registration number TW 6120) in his garage at his home, Shirley, near Oak Tree Corner, in Billericay and locked the doors. He left some of his medical paraphernalia in the vehicle. Five hours later he went to bed, but when he went to the garage in the morning the car was gone.

At 7.30 am on 27 September Albert McDougall left his home in Brixton on his way to work. As he left via the back door his

This blue Morris Cowley was stolen from Dr Edward Richardson Lovell in Billericay. Essex Police Museum

way was partially blocked by a car. Partially disabled, he was annoyed that the car was there but managed to squeeze by it. On his return that night, the vehicle was still there so he rang the police to complain. At 6.45 pm Detective Sergeant Charles Hearn foolishly drove the car to Brixton police station where it could be examined – foolishly because it meant his fingerprints were on the steering wheel. A search was made of the car and a bullet casing marked R.L.I.V. was found under the front seat. Spots of blood were discovered on the offside running board. Dr Lovell travelled to Brixton police station where he confirmed the car was his and told the police about the missing medical equipment.

About an hour and a half before Albert McDougall was inconvenienced by the car blocking his way to work, William Ward, a car engineer from Warley Road, Brentwood, was in his own car delivering post to sub mail offices in Romford and

Abridge when he spotted a figure huddled by the side of the Ongar-Romford road. The man was leaning against a grassy bank with his legs outstretched. Mr Ward went to fetch help and knocked up Albert Perritt who lived at Rose Cottage in Howe Green. The two men recognised the sitting man as PC 489 George Gutteridge – they also noted that he was dead. They moved him so that any oncoming cars would not run over his legs.

George William Gutteridge was born in Winbotsham, Downham Market, Norfolk on 29 July 1889 and joined the Essex constabulary on 5 April 1910. He stayed in the job until April 1918 when he resigned to join the Army. He served in the Machine Gun Corps for ten months where he served under Oscar Berry Tompkins. On 23 February 1919, he rejoined the Essex constabulary and was posted to Grays. On 14 March 1922, he transferred to the Epping Division and was assigned a beat that included Stapleford Abbots, Kelvedon Hatch, Lambourne End and Stamford Rivers. He was based at Stapleford Abbots where he lived at 2 Townley Cottages with his wife, Rose Annette Emmerline, and their two children, Muriel, aged twelve, and Alfred, aged four. Tall and moustachioed, PC Gutteridge was a popular local figure and could frequently be found drinking in the *Royal Oak* with the people he policed. He drank often and well, and on more than one occasion he was discovered drunk in a hedge after last orders.

On 26 September 1927, he was back at home by 6 pm and spent the evening with his family. When his wife went to bed at 11 pm, he reluctantly donned his uniform and went out on patrol. His family would never see him alive again. It was PC Gutteridge's usual habit to meet his opposite number at Lambourne End, PC Sydney Taylor, at 3 am for a chat and a catch-up at Howe Green, which was a mile from PC Gutteridge's cottage and about a mile and three quarters from PC Taylor's. They met and caught up on the local villains before going their separate ways at five past three. PC Taylor was home and in bed by 4.30 am.

When PC Gutteridge's body was examined Detective Inspector John Crockford noted that there were 'two holes which appeared consistent with the entry of two large bullets' and the base of the skull was 'practically blown away'. There was a stub of a pencil in his hand and his notebook lay on the floor nearby. His truncheon and whistle were still in his pockets and there did not appear to be any signs of a struggle.

At 9 am Dr Robert Woodhouse arrived from Romford and pronounced death extinct at the scene. Then the body was moved to the coach house of the *Royal Oak*, one hundred yards from the Gutteridge family home.

The police supposed that after leaving PC Taylor, PC Gutteridge had flagged down a passing car and, as he noted its particulars, he was shot twice in the face. As he lay on the floor he was shot in each eye.

The chief constable of Essex, Captain John A Unett, asked Scotland Yard for help and Detective Chief Inspector James Berrett was put in charge of the case. He brought Detective Sergeant John Harris with him and the two policemen arrived in Stapleford Abbots on the afternoon of 27 September.

On 28 September Dr Woodhouse carried out an autopsy on

The spot where PC Gutteridge was murdered. Paul Donnelley

PC Gutteridge and discovered seven wounds in his head: two in the left cheek, one in the right cheek, one in the right side of the neck, one below each eye and a final one at the back of the skull. He surmised that the holes in the left cheek and under the eyes were entry wounds and the others exit wounds. He said that one of the wounds in the left cheek would not have been in itself fatal, but the other severed the carotid artery and would have led to death by haemorrhage in about two minutes. Then the doctor turned his attention to the wounds in the eyes. Both of these would have been instantly fatal. The doctor found that one of the bullets was still lodged in PC Gutteridge's skull.

PC Gutteridge was buried in Warley Cemetery with full police honours and the address was given by the Bishop of Barking, Dr James Theodore Inskip. A year later, a seven-foot-high cross was placed on the grave bearing the inscription 'In proud memory of George William Gutteridge, Police Constable, Essex Constabulary, who met his death in the performance of his duty on September 27th 1927'.

But who had killed the policeman?

It fell to James Berrett, who bore more than a passing resemblance to King Edward VII, to investigate. A vastly experienced policeman, he had joined the Metropolitan Police Force in 1893 and transferred to New Scotland Yard in 1926. When he arrived in Stapleford Abbots, it was to head the most extensive police investigation in Britain up to that time.

DCI Berrett learned that a car had been stolen at 2.30 am and, working out the time that PC Gutteridge would have taken to walk to the meeting with PC Taylor and where his body was found, death was estimated to have taken place at 3.35 am.

DCI Berrett's investigation focused on known criminals. Many were taken into custody and at least two confessed to crimes that were not being investigated. One name topped the list, typed in alphabetical order. Frederick Guy Browne.

Frederick Guy Browne was born as Leo Browne in Catford probably in 1881 (he himself did not know the exact date). His first conviction was in 1911. He had taken to stealing bicycles,

PC Gutteridge's service record. Becky
Latchford

dismantling them and selling off the parts. He was caught after he forgot to remove the serial number of one and was sentenced to two months' hard labour. Released in January 1912, Browne was back inside almost immediately for burglary, sentenced to 12 months' hard labour. In April 1912 he was convicted at Buckinghamshire Quarter Sessions and was released in February 1913. In May 1913 he appeared at Oxford City Quarter Sessions charged with stealing a bicycle and received another 12 months' hard labour. He was released in March 1914. On 4 September 1915, he married Caroline, a girl in service. A daughter was born and by all accounts Browne was a devoted father and a faithful husband. In March 1917 he joined the Army, becoming a sapper in the Royal Engineers. On 5 November 1918 he was dishonourably discharged for stealing a motorbike and sent to prison.

In 1919, Browne was released from prison and landed a job as a mechanic in Clapham. The family stayed there for two years before they moved to Eastwood, near Southend, in 1921. He made a living stealing cars and clocking them. On Christmas Eve 1922, he and some colleagues were arrested and charged with conspiracy to defraud and forgery. He was tried at the Old Bailey and sentenced to four years' penal servitude.

He began his sentence at Parkhust on the Isle of Wight, where he quickly gained a reputation as a thug. He beat up a prison officer and smashed up his cell. He even removed bricks from the wall of his cell so he could chat to the next inmate more easily. He refused to carry out his hard labour and was placed on a bread and water diet for fifty-seven-days in a bid to break him. He was sent to Dartmoor where he served his full sentence without remission.

It was at Dartmoor that he met William Henry Kennedy, the man with whose name he was to be linked in criminal history.

On 30 March 1927, Browne was released from prison and immediately went back to a life of crime. In June, he rented premises at 7a Northcote Road, Lavender Hill, south London, which were big enough for seven cars. That summer he was joined by Kennedy.

William Henry Kennedy was born in Ayrshire in 1891. After a career in the Army, he too began a life of crime. He was convicted of larceny, theft, drunk and disorderly behaviour, and twice for indecent exposure. On his release from prison, he rejoined the Army. He was dishonourably discharged in October 1917.

In January 1928, Browne was arrested for the theft of a Vauxhall car in Tooting in November 1927. As they searched his car police found guns, bullets, a fake driving licence and a stocking mask with holes cut in it for mouth and eyes.

DCI Berrett arrived to question Browne about the night that PC Gutteridge was killed.

When the police searched Browne's home, they discovered a doctor's speculum in a chest of drawers and on the mantelpiece was a roll of adhesive surgical plaster. They also found, wrapped in a handkerchief, two dozen .22 cartridges.

Next, Browne was questioned by Detective Sergeant Harris. Browne put down the reason for carrying a gun as fear of being robbed while delivering cars as he had been during the war. He had the medical supplies in case of an accident and claimed to have bought them in pharmacies around the country. He vehemently denied ever having driven around Essex late at night or knowing anything about the killing of PC Gutteridge. 'I have no connection with the murder...and personally I am not

Bullets recovered by police investigating the murder of PC Gutteridge. Essex
Police Museum

interested because it does not affect me', he claimed.

As they interviewed him, policemen continued to search his
home and the doctor's car and recovered numerous items from
robberies perpetrated by Browne as well as discovering four
handguns. The next day Browne was questioned again and
during the interview the police produced three of the four guns.
He made a second statement admitting to having guns and
ammunition, 'but I decline to give any explanation of where I
got them'.

On 23 January 1928 at 1.45 pm, Detective Inspector William Barker formally charged Guy Browne with stealing a Vauxhall car from a garage at 1 Franciscan Road, Tooting, south London on 12 or 13 November 1927. Browne continued to deny that he had stolen the car and such was the scarcity of cars on the road in those days that the owner, Bridget Hulton, was unable to even identify the vehicle as hers.

On 25 January, William Kennedy was arrested after a gun battle with Detective Sergeant William Mattinson in Liverpool. The charge was 'being concerned with a man named Browne, now in custody, in stealing a Vauxhall motor car from Tooting, London, in November last'. There was no mention of PC Gutteridge's murder. Kennedy breathed a temporary sigh of relief. The next day Kennedy was taken to London via train, arriving at Euston at 6 pm. He was then taken to Scotland Yard where questioning began an hour later.

DCI Berrett said, 'You are being detained on a charge of being concerned in stealing a Vauxhall motor car but I have been making enquiries for some time past respecting the murder of PC Gutteridge at Essex. Can you give me any information about the occurrence?'.

Kennedy replied, 'I may be able to tell you something, but let me consider awhile'. He then asked to see his wife, Patricia, who had also travelled down from Liverpool. The police agreed and Kennedy told her that he was being questioned about the murder of PC Gutteridge. She asked if he had done it and Kennedy replied, 'No I didn't but I was there and know who did'. Kennedy then told his wife that if he were convicted for murder he would hang and she would be a widow, but if he were merely found guilty for being an accomplice, he would receive a long prison sentence. Would she wait for him?

She replied, 'Yes, love, I will wait for you a long time'.

'What shall I do then?'

'Tell these gentlemen the truth of what took place.'

Kennedy was then cautioned before he began speaking at 7.15 pm. His nineteen-page statement was taken down by

Sergeant Harris and was completed at 11 pm.

Kennedy described himself as a thirty-seven-year-old compositor of no fixed abode. He told the police that he had met Browne in Dartmoor and that he had been contacted when he was released. He went on to say that on the morning of 26 September Browne had asked him to go to Billericay where he intended to steal a car. They caught a train from Liverpool Street to Southend but a dog's barking scared them off from their original mission. They hung around until 11 pm by which time they had reached the London road and spotted a house with a garage.

The house belonged to Dr Lovell.

According to Kennedy, they checked the level of the petrol tank before pushing the car away from the house and then they kept to the side roads where they were stopped by PC Gutteridge. The policeman asked for identification or proof of ownership. Kennedy said that the car was his. PC Gutteridge asked for the registration number which Kennedy was able to tell him.

The policeman then pulled out his notebook to take notes, according to Kennedy, when there was a loud report.

Kennedy said that he asked Browne, 'What have you done?', then:

> I got out and went round to the policeman who was lying on his back, and Browne came over and said 'I'll finish the bugger', and I said 'Don't shoot anymore, the man's dying', as he was groaning. The policeman's eyes were open and Browne, addressing him, said 'What are you looking at me like that for?' and, stooping down, shot him at close range through both eyes. There were only two shots fired. Browne then said 'Let's get back to the car'.

Kennedy then claimed that Browne told him to reload the Webley revolver but, in his excitement, he dropped an empty shell in the car.

The two men, said Kennedy, dumped the car and smashed

most of Dr Lovell's equipment. Kennedy then added that he had forgotten to mention that in the fog Browne had driven the car into a tree, damaging, he thought, the nearside wing.

Kennedy finished his statement by saying that he knew Browne owned two Webley revolvers and a Smith & Wesson but that he had never seen the latter weapon.

Kennedy said that what he had said was the truth and signed a statement to that effect.

On 27 January, Kennedy was taken to Cannon Row police station and charged with stealing a Vauxhall car. He denied all knowledge of the offence.

Three days later, Browne and Kennedy appeared before the magistrate John Brown Sandbach, KC, at South Western police court. The two men were remanded in custody in Brixton prison for a fortnight.

On 6 February 1928, at 8.30 am, DCI Berrett formally charged Browne and Kennedy with the murder of PC Gutteridge. Kennedy was silent but Browne replied, 'It's absurd. I know nothing about it'.

DCI Berrett handed each man a copy of the statement made by the other. Later that day, the two men appeared in court where they were remanded in custody until their trial.

As Browne and Kennedy awaited the start of the trial, the police began a careful forensic examination of the weaponry and bullets found in the stolen car, at the murder scene, in PC Gutteridge, about Kennedy's person and at Browne's home.

On 13 February, the two men appeared before Lavender Hill magistrates. Sir Travers Humphrey led the prosecution aided by Henry Delacombe Roome, while Edmund O'Connor appeared for Browne and Oscar Berry Tompkins, PC Gutteridge's former Army colleague, represented Kennedy.

Mrs Browne and Mrs Kennedy sat together in court, both dressed in funereal black.

Sir Travers Humphrey opened the case for the Crown outlining how the two defendants stole Dr Lovell's car.

Edmund O'Connor objected when Sir Travers Humphrey referred to the statement given by Browne to police. The lawyer said that the caution received by his client had been improperly administered. The magistrate, John Brown Sandbach, overruled the objection. Oscar Berry Tompkins stood to object when Sir Travers referred to Kennedy's arrest and the statement he made to police claiming that evidence against one man could not be used to implicate the other.

Mr Sandbach agreed: 'I shall not accept it as evidence against Browne, and if the only evidence against Browne is a statement by Kennedy, I shall not commit Browne for trial'.

Mr Tompkins then added that Kennedy had been forced by the police to make a statement and Mr Sandbach said that if he was persuaded that the statement had indeed been made under duress, he would exclude it as evidence.

The two men were remanded in custody until 21 February for legal argument to be heard. Sir Travers Humphrey was appointed a judge and dropped out of the case and Mr Roome took over as lead counsel.

Mr O'Connor asked DCI Berrett if he had suspected Browne of being involved in the murder of PC Gutteridge after his admission about firearms. The policeman perjured himself and denied that he had, claiming that he was merely one of many suspects. In his memoirs, he confessed that he had indeed suspected Browne from the beginning.

DCI Berrett faced a barrage of questions from both counsels and maintained that Kennedy had not been emotionally or physically bullied during the course of his police interview and gave his statement willingly.

After considering what he had seen and heard, Mr Sandbach decided that the Kennedy statement could be admitted as evidence. He believed that anyone who knew DCI Berrett could not believe that he could be anything but truthful – a naïve assumption.

On 3 April 1928, the two men were committed for trial at the Central Criminal Court at the Old Bailey.

'One of the most dramatic murder trials of recent years', as the press labelled it, opened on 23 April. The public gallery of forty was packed and several of the seats were occupied by celebrities. Queues for the seats began early, long before the court opened at 10am.

Presiding over the proceedings was seventy-seven-year-old Mr Justice Avory (born at 3 Pitts Place, Southwark, London, on 31 August 1851 as Horace Edmond Avery) who had a reputation as a hanging judge. He was also the recipient of more threatening letters than any other judge. He treated them as a joke and kept them in a scrapbook.

Sir (Frank) Boyd Merriman, KC (born at Knutsford, 28 April 1880) led the prosecution assisted by H D Roome and Enid Rosser, making history as the first woman barrister to appear at an Old Bailey murder trial.

Guy Browne was defended by E F Lever. Thirty years earlier, Lever had defended the killer Albert Milsom, one of the Muswell Hill Murderers; Horace Avory had been the prosecuting counsel. Frank Powell defended William Kennedy. The case was regarded as so important that Sir Archibald Bodkin, the Director of Public Prosecutions, sat next to the clerk of the court and Sir Ernley Blackwell, the Permanent Under-Secretary at the Home Office, was also present.

Mr Justice Avory opened proceedings by asking if the three women jurors would like to be excused. None did.

The clerk of the court then read the charges against Browne and Kennedy and asked if they pleaded guilty or not guilty. Both men issued pleas of not guilty.

The jury was then sent out and Mr Lever asked the judge to allow separate trials, mainly due to Kennedy's statement implicating Browne. He also mentioned the methodology of how the statement was obtained. Mr Lever referred to the Thompson and Bywaters appeal before the Lord Chief Justice who said: 'No doubt, where the defence of one accused person is to incriminate another, there is good reason for not trying them together'.

Sir Boyd Merriman demurred, saying that since the two

men had been engaged on the crime together, they should be tried together. He said, 'It would be farcical and redundant for a considerable mass of detailed evidence, apart from [Kennedy's] statement to have to be rehearsed twice over before two juries'.

The judge agreed. 'In my opinion no sufficient reason has been shown for making the order which has been asked for in this case, and I must refuse the application.' On their return to the courtroom the jury was sworn in.

Sir Boyd Merriman opened the case for the prosecution and outlined the case as seen by the Crown, from the theft of Dr Lovell's car to the murder of PC Gutteridge to the arrest of the accused. He returned to the vexatious matter of Kennedy's statement. 'Let me say at once, and forgive me if I say it again, that the statement is evidence against Kennedy alone. It is not to be taken as evidence against Browne.'

He said that even if there was uncertainty as to who had pulled the trigger the two men had acted in concert and thus were equally culpable.

Statements given by Browne and Kennedy were read in their entirety to the court. Sir Boyd Merriman drew the jury's attention to the fact that the gun had been reloaded thus showing that:

> these two men were determined by any means to resist anybody who opposed their escape. Try to picture to yourselves the mentality of a man who, according to his own statement, had seen a fellow man murdered in cold blood and is prepared to reload the revolver and hand it back to the man sitting next to him in the driver's seat of the car.

Merriman finished by relating how Kennedy had pulled a gun on Detective Sergeant William Mattinson who tried to arrest him (and succeeded).

It was the turn of the Crown to produce its prosecution witnesses. The first into the box was Rose Gutteridge, the policeman's widow. She told how she had last seen her husband at Romford mortuary and left the witness stand in tears.

The second witness was PC Sydney Taylor who said that he had met PC Gutteridge the night of the murder and left him at 3.25 am. One of the odd things about PC Taylor's testimony was his claim not to have heard the shots that killed PC Gutteridge. Yet he could not have been have been more than three-quarters of a mile away. PC Gutteridge was killed 638 yards from where he had left PC Taylor. PC Taylor would have been near Battles Hall in Hook Lane. Even more oddly, he was not questioned at the trial as to why he had not heard the commotion.

Another witness, Lady Decies, said that she had been woken by a car passing her house opposite the *Royal Oak* pub on the Ongar-Romford road between 3 and 4 am. It must have been the car driven by Browne and Kennedy but it was heading towards Romford. Kennedy claimed that it was travelling in the opposite direction. It must have been the Browne/Kennedy car because if it had been another it would have passed the murder scene within seconds and we know that did not happen.

Bizarrely, Lady Decies was not called to testify and no one sought to explain the apparent car discrepancy.

The next two witnesses, William Ward and Alfred Perritt, repeated what they had said at the magistrate's court. The next people to enter the witness box were policemen.

Frank Powell opened the defence for William Kennedy by stating that there was no case to answer. He claimed that the prosecution had not proved that Kennedy was aware that Browne was armed on the night of 27 September 1927. 'I submit that in a charge of this sort', he said, 'even though it is proved *prima facie* that the two defendants were together at the time, it must be proved by the prosecution that Kennedy knew that Browne had a revolver and would use it upon the night in question'.

The judge was not impressed. 'I think it is better to say no more than to say there is, in my opinion, a case against Kennedy for Kennedy to answer.'

Mr Lever stated that Browne's defence would be based on the fact that he was entirely ignorant of the events surrounding PC Gutteridge's killing. 'It is my terribly difficult duty to extract from your minds the impression created by the statement made by Kennedy. I do not ask for sympathy. I demand justice.'

He went on to claim that on the night of the killing Browne was at home with his wife. He did own the pistols but had never fired them and merely owned them for his own protection.

Mr Powell refused to let his client go into the witness box. Mr Lever had no such qualms. However, as Frederick Guy Browne walked to the box he turned to Mr Justice Avory and said, 'Your Lordship, I want to swear different to this; it says here "The whole truth"; I shall never know the whole truth about this; how can I swear the whole truth?'

Mr Justice Avory replied, 'Are you going to take the oath or not?'

'Yes', replied Browne, 'but I do not know the whole truth; I cannot tell the whole truth'.

'You will either take the oath in that form or not at all.'

'It is awkward. How can I tell the whole truth? I can only tell the whole truth as far as I am concerned.'

'You must make up your mind. You will either take the oath in that form or not at all.'

'It seems wrong. That is what I am looking at.'

'I will not have any more time wasted. You must do one thing or the other.'

'If I take it, is it an oath?'

'That is the oath which you are required by law to take if you intend to give evidence upon oath; if you do not...'

'I do not intend to give evidence on this oath.'

'If so...'

'I do on oath.'

'Then you must take the oath in that form.'

'I do. "I swear by Almighty God that the evidence". That is not right.'

The judge became exasperated. 'You can read, can't you?'

'I can read distinctly, quite clear.'

'Very well, read that.'

'I swear by Almighty God that the evidence I shall give shall be the truth, the whole truth and nothing but the truth.'

Mr Lever sought to explain his client's behaviour thinking that the jury might not understand it.

'I can tell the truth but how can I tell the whole truth of something I do not know? I can tell the court as much of the truth as I know, and nothing but the truth', he said.

'That, I think, the jury will now quite understand', said Mr Lever.

The judge was not quite as understanding. 'Do not make these observations. It is not for you to say whether the jury will understand. I do not understand it.'

His lawyer tried to intervene but again Browne said that he could not tell the truth of something he did not know.

Mr Justice Avory lost his temper. 'You are not to make speeches to the jury. Attend to the questions and answer them.'

The arguments cannot have played favourably with the jury who saw him as an awkward, irascible, argumentative man.

Finally, Mr Lever began to question his client and Browne said that he had been at home on the night that PC Gutteridge was killed. He had been out once to take his wife from one place to another but had never ventured to Essex.

Browne said that the 'medical instruments' were, in fact, tools that he used in his job as a mechanic. The doctor's speculum found in a chest of drawers at his home was, so Browne claimed, used for seeing if engines were clogged up with carbon. A pair of forceps was used for handling fuel jets. He used the anaesthetic when he needed to pull a metal splinter out of his hand with the fine tweezers.

Questioned about the guns, Browne said that he kept them in the garage and that Kennedy could easily have had access to them. He dismissed Kennedy's statement as 'a fairytale from beginning to end'.

He said that he had tried to look after Kennedy because the

latter was a drunkard but that in the end he had had no option but to sack him in December, only for Kennedy to reappear in the New Year.

Mr Powell rose to his feet and said that he did not plan to cross-examine Browne as long as he did not dispute the fact that Kennedy could not drive.

Browne not only disputed that but said that he had seen Kennedy drive at least three different cars. It must be remembered that Browne's alibi would be considerably weakened if it could be proved that Kennedy could not drive.

'I put it to you', said Mr Powell, 'that he has never driven a car at all'.

'You can put it to me. I will put it to you, why does he take a driver's licence out? People do not take a licence out to drive wheelbarrows', retorted Browne.

Evidence was submitted that proved that Kennedy could drive, albeit rather badly.

The cross-examination moved on. Browne said that he had given Kennedy a Savage automatic around 7 October 1927 and had been given a Webley in return. However, when Mr Powell attempted to ask about the two Webley revolvers the court dissolved into confusion and it was clear that the jury had no idea which gun was being discussed.

Mr Justice Avory asked Browne if he would agree that the gun found in the car was the murder weapon but Browne demurred. 'How am I to know that?' he asked.

'You must take it, it is so.'

'It is not very fair to me, is it? I must take it for granted?'

Browne said that his weapon, bought at Tilbury Docks, was going rusty but was unsure which gun was being referred to by the court. When he was asked by Mr Powell if the murder weapon was the one that was in Kennedy's possession, Browne said that he did not know.

The judge said that Browne had said that the newer gun, the murder weapon, was the one that Browne had bought in Tilbury but Browne disagreed.

The pistol used to kill PC Gutteridge. Essex Police Museum

'I did not. I said the one that began to get rusty I got from a sailor; if you have twisted it round it is not my fault.'

The judge again lost his temper but if the court had referred to Browne's sworn statement they would have read that the older gun, the rusty one, was the one that he had bought in Tilbury. Browne was quite specific on this, as well he might be since his very life lay in the balance.

The next witnesses confirmed Browne's whereabouts on the Sunday preceding the killing of PC Gutteridge and his explanation for the 'medical instruments'.

Caroline Browne said that her husband had been at home all night and confirmed that Kennedy could drive. Her evidence concluded day three of the trial.

On day four she was recalled to the witness box and questioned by Sir Boyd Merriman. She again corroborated her husband's testimony about his whereabouts on the night of the murder.

If one expects a loyal spouse to back up whatever her husband says, then there must be another person to corroborate that statement.

There was just such a person.

The Brownes' landlady at 33a Sisters Avenue, Clapham, Mary Siddals, had told police that she had heard the couple moving about in their flat and made them a cup of tea. However, Mrs Siddals' statement did not contain these pertinent facts nor were they mentioned in court. Had they been, Frederick Guy Browne's innocence would have been confirmed – he could not have been in Essex killing a policeman.

Detective Sergeant John Harris was recalled to the stand and asked if Mrs Browne had read and signed her statement and whether he had read it. His answer was unsatisfactory. 'Parts were read, not the whole.'

It is obvious that the police took statements that only benefited their case against Browne and Kennedy and omitted those parts of the evidence that did not fit in with their thesis.

Evidence from Lady Decies, Mrs Siddals and Mrs Browne was all conveniently (for the police) ignored.

Mr Lever announced that while his client did not wish to go into the witness box, where his criminal record would have become known (as was then possible), he would, instead, make a statement from the dock.

Kennedy leaned on the rail of the dock and said that his statement to Inspector Berrett was 'absolutely true…I had not the slightest idea on the night of the murder that Browne was carrying a revolver. The first intimation I got of it was when I heard the two shots fired. It was too late then for me to do anything to stop it.'

Kennedy also denied threatening Detective Sergeant William Mattinson in Liverpool when he was arrested. He finished by saying that he was completely innocent of the murder and expressing sympathy for Mrs Gutteridge. In fact, Kennedy's statement was a tissue of lies from start to finish.

The lawyers then made their closing statements. Mr Lever said that when they read Kennedy's statement they would have thought the police 'have got the right men and Browne is the worst of them'. He added that what Kennedy had said against Browne was not, in fact, evidence against Browne. Mr Lever said that the evidence against Browne was 'pitiful' and that it would have been better if the two men had had separate trials.

Again, Mr Justice Avory lost his temper. 'You have no right to say that.'

Mr Lever said that he had not meant to cause offence but that the main evidence against Browne was Kennedy's statement and that if it had not been used and there had been separate trials, Browne's chances of acquittal would have been much greater.

He admitted that although Browne was 'not a lovable man' that did not make him a cold-blooded murderer. 'There was no evidence that Browne had used the revolver which killed Gutteridge; a revolver that Browne neither owned nor possessed at that time.'

He finished:

[Browne] stands before you in his rights as a man, a human being like yourselves, endowed with the same faculties, crowned with the same spiritual attributes, but near him hovers the dark angel of death. He asks you for no sympathy, but he does demand justice, and if you can throw off this burden of prejudice, if you can by a superhuman effort rise to the high place of abstract justice, he will await your decision not in despair but in hopeful anticipation of receiving, at long last, a verdict of acquittal at your hands.

Mr Powell began by stating that Kennedy had not given evidence because all that was needed to prove his innocence was before the court. To prove Kennedy's guilt, it was necessary to establish that he knew that Browne was armed when the two went out. Since, Mr Powell said, Kennedy did not know that Browne had a gun with him until he heard the shots he could not have known that he was armed and, therefore, was not and could not have been a party to the shooting.

Both defence counsels had spent much of their time in court attempting to damn the other as well as defending their own client. Consequently, the Solicitor-General did not have to spend much time on his closing statement. He finished, 'I am bound to submit on behalf of the prosecution that there is abundant evidence on which you should infer the guilt of both these prisoners'.

On day five of the trial Mr Justice Avory began his summation. He began by telling them that they must base their verdict on the evidence that they had heard in court and not on any preconceived ideas or notions that they may have had. 'I would remind you once more, although you may be tired of hearing it, that the statement made by the accused Kennedy is evidence against Kennedy alone, and is not evidence against Browne.' He also advised the jury not to be swayed by the result of their deliberations i.e. that both men would face the death penalty if found guilty. Thirdly, he said that the prosecution had to prove the men's guilt. It was not for the accused to prove their innocence.

The judge then moved onto the subject of the separate trials and said that even if they had been tried separately Kennedy would have been called as a witness for the Crown against Browne. This was Mr Lever's point. By not allowing separate trials the judge had prevented his cross-examination of Kennedy.

At 12.52 pm the judge ended his summing-up and sent the jury to consider their verdicts. There was a buzz in the courtroom as no one left their seats. Browne and Kennedy were taken to the cells to await their fates. Their wives stayed in the court although after thirty minutes Mrs Kennedy broke down in tears.

At 3.10 pm the jury filed back into the courtroom. Police moved to lock and bar the doors to the court. There were rumours that the judge's life had been threatened.

The prisoners were brought up. Browne was first and he

smiled at someone who waved to him from the public gallery. He looked relaxed. Kennedy appeared looking tense. Warders stood between the two men.

The clerk of the court rose and asked the foreman of the jury to stand. 'Members of the jury, have you agreed upon your verdict?'

'We have.'

'Do you find the accused Frederick Guy Browne guilty or not guilty of the murder of George William Gutteridge?'

'Guilty, sir.'

Browne did not show any emotion.

'Do you find the accused William Henry Kennedy guilty or not guilty of the murder of George William Gutteridge?'

'Guilty, sir.'

Kennedy stumbled and grasped hold of the dock rail to steady himself.

Asked if they had anything to say, Browne said:

The court, as you say, according to law, has found me guilty of wilful murder; I cannot alter the court, I would not desire to. I admit here now that counsel has acted very nicely and very fairly as far as I am concerned. I admit I would not wish to be tried by a better judge, but the jury have had stuff given to them that is not genuine; it is the fault of the way it has been put together. It will come out later on that I had nothing to do with it, but I am not going to argue the point. I am not going to try and prove it to you, because the simple reason is that there is something hanging over my head, that if I got off this I should get penal servitude for something else, which is far worse than what is offered me. I am quite content to leave it, but I am not guilty according to the One Above that knows. I am not guilty, but the court says I am. I am quite content, my conscience is clear.

Kennedy said:

My lord, nothing I can say now will alter the verdict which has been arrived at. I am going to say this. It was pre-ordained. It was fate and you, my lord, however fairly you may have tried me, and members of the jury, are mere accessories of that fate. I say it in no mere spirit of bravado when I said that I am not afraid to die, but I meet it willingly, because I have the certain knowledge that in the hereafter I will be reunited for all eternity to the one darling girl who has stuck to me all through this trouble. I wish to return my thanks for the able way in which I have been defended.

Mr Justice Avory sat still as his clerk placed the black silk square – the black cap – on his head.

He pronounced sentence of death on the two men.

Browne was taken to Pentonville and Kennedy to Wandsworth.

While waiting for sentence to be carried out Browne tried to commit suicide three times, once by hanging himself and then by cutting his throat. He even tried to go on a hunger strike and had to be force fed.

On 22 May 1928, appeals from both men were dismissed.

To show that cheque book journalism is not a new phenomenon, the *News of the World* offered a friend of Browne £2,000 for information on him.

While awaiting his death Kennedy converted to Roman Catholicism.

At 9 am on Thursday, 31 May 1928, Browne was hanged at Pentonville by Robert Orridge Baxter, assisted by Henry Pollard. The night before his execution Browne wrote a letter to the London press and gave his return address as the 'Prison Mortuary'.

Thomas William Pierrepoint and Robert Wilson dispatched Kennedy at Wandsworth.

On the day of their deaths Browne and Kennedy were buried within the precepts of the prisons in which they died. Their bodies remain there to this day.

In 1992 the files on the case held at the Public Records Office at Kew were mysteriously destroyed.

Mr Justice Avory died on 13 June 1935 of heart failure, at the

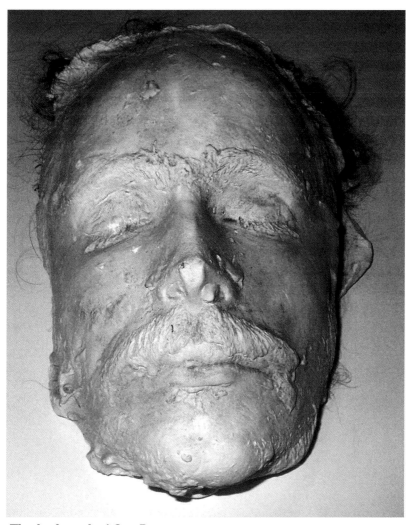

The death mask of Guy Browne. Becky Latchford

Dormy House Club, Rye, Sussex.

William Barker retired from the police in 1937.

James Berrett's autobiography was published on 7 April 1932. He died of a heart attack on 24 May 1940. He left £1,611.

Little is known of Caroline Browne's fate.

Patricia Kennedy married the taxi driver who took her to Wandsworth for her husband's execution.

The memorial to PC Gutteridge near Havering-atte-Bower. Paul Donnelley

William Mattinson died in 1969 aged 77.

Sir (Frank) Boyd Merriman, KC (later Baron Merriman), died in London on 18 January 1962.

Edmund O'Connor was declared bankrupt in June 1936 and again in 1937. He was convicted of fraud and forgery and sentenced to seven years in prison.

Henry Delacombe Roome was killed in a car crash at Retford on 8 June 1930.

Oscar Berry Tompkins died aged 85 in 1970 at his bungalow which overlooked Hove golf course.

Some locals believe that PC Gutteridge's ghost still patrols his beat.

Chapter 12

Who Killed
Pamela Coventry?

'He was shocked to see the naked
body of a young girl'

Elm Park was built on agricultural land in the mid-1930s and its creators called it the 'Wonder Town of Homes'. Fourteen point three miles east-northeast of the centre of London, it was, at the time, the largest private housing development in the United Kingdom. Homes in Elm Park cost about £395 with a mortgage of eleven shillings per week.

It is served by the District Line and the station opened on 13 May 1935, and Elm Park shopping parade was completed in 1939.

In that year it had a population of 90,800, which the local council reported was growing steadily.

Elm Park Underground Station, opened in 1935, serves a thriving community. Paul Donnelley

Two years previously, the Coventry family – widower Stanley, an electrician, second wife Edith and his eight-year-old daughter Pamela – moved into Diban Avenue in Elm Park, just off the optimistically named Park Avenue and a stone's throw from the station.

In December 1938, the family upped sticks and moved to Morecambe Close on the other side of the railway. Mrs Coventry had engineered the move alone as her husband had been working in Scunthorpe since the previous month.

In December 1938 the Coventry family moved to Morecambe Close. Paul Donnelley

Pamela Doreen Coventry was born on 12 February 1929 and her mother died while she was still a toddler. In 1935 her father had remarried. Pamela was friendly and popular at school although she had a tendency to be shy with strangers, no bad thing then or now.

Benhurst Primary School in Elm Park, attended by Pamela Coventry. Paul Donnelley

She attended the primary school on Benhurst Avenue, near to her old home on Diban Avenue. Each day she came home for lunch and strolled back to school. It was a simple route – up Lancaster Drive, left onto Coronation Drive, through The Broadway and right into Benhurst Avenue.

Every Tuesday, she took music lessons in a house on Diban Avenue which she knew well, having lived there, and it had the added bonus of being a minute or so from school.

On Tuesday, 3 January 1939, Pamela went for her music lesson as usual and was back home by 6.30 pm. She asked her stepmother if she could run an errand for a man who lived on Coronation Drive but when questioned Pamela admitted that she had only just met the man as she returned from the lesson. Mrs Coventry refused to let her stepdaughter go.

Just over a fortnight later on Wednesday, 18 January, Pamela came home from school at her usual time of 12.45 pm. Around half an hour later, she left her home to go back to school.

That day the weather was cold and Mrs Coventry made sure her stepdaughter was wrapped up. Under Pamela's arm she carried a brown paper bag holding her dancing shoes.

She had arranged to meet two friends at 1.30 pm by the railway bridge. Mrs Coventry waved as Pamela set off and turned into Coronation Drive. Somewhere between being waved off and the railway bridge, Pamela Coventry simply disappeared.

Her friends waited but there was no sign of Pamela. Thinking she was not well or perhaps playing truant, they went to school and the teacher marked Pamela absent when the register was called.

There was no sense of alarm until Mrs Coventry came to collect her stepdaughter at the school gates. She asked among the teachers and pupils but no one had any idea where Pamela was. Mrs Coventry went to the police and reported her stepdaughter missing. By 10.30 pm there was still no sign and it began to rain heavily which made searching for the little girl very difficult.

At 10.30 am the next day Charles J Horsman, a night watchman of North Street, Hornchurch, was cycling down Wood Lane which is to the south of Morecambe Close. In those days the road was bordered on one side by a deep ditch and Mr Horsman happened to glance into the ditch and spotted a pale object at the bottom. Curiosity got the better of him and he dismounted and went to investigate. He was shocked to see the naked body of a young girl lying on a rotting mattress. The child had been stripped of her warm winter clothes and was clad only in a petticoat. She had also been bound with what appeared to be electrical cable.

Mr Horsman raised the alarm at the home of the wing commander of the local RAF station who called the police. A doctor pronounced the child dead at the scene and hypothesised that death had occurred several hours earlier. He also noted that the girl had been subjected to a brutal sexual assault. She was quickly identified as Pamela Coventry.

The local police called in Scotland Yard. The Metropolitan and Essex police forces and the RAF searched the locale for

Pamela Coventry's body (white bundle) can be seen in the ditch on the left of the picture. Essex Police Museum

clues and, in particular, Pamela's missing clothes.

The eminent pathologist, Sir Bernard Spilsbury, carried out the autopsy on poor Pamela, assisted by Dr Francis Camps. Their findings revealed that Pamela had been punched on the jaw and fell hitting the other side of her face, the left. He added that although these injuries were not enough to cause death they did probably knock her out so that when she was raped she was unconscious. Death was caused by strangulation and blood was discovered in Pamela's right nostril.

Sir Bernard also noted that Pamela's corpse was clean giving him reason to believe that she was killed indoors. He also revealed that she had died within an hour of her last meal, which indicated that death had occurred within half an hour of leaving home. Further, although the mattress in the ditch was wet from the heavy rain, Pamela's body was dry which meant that she had been dumped there after the rain had ceased.

The cable with which Pamela had been trussed was fifteen feet of seven-strand black copper insulated flex. Attached to it along its length was creosoted or tarred string. It seemed likely that it had been used in a garden, perhaps to tie up runner beans or other climbing plants. There was also a piece of green cable with string attached and when the body was laid out a hand-rolled cigarette butt was discovered pressed between the thigh and chest.

The police began trying to track the manufacturer of the cable and discovered that although the green one was still in the shops, the black variety had not been made for more than a dozen years. Pictures of both were taken and published in the national press and although the police were inundated with calls, none bore fruit.

As is usual in murder enquiries, especially high profile ones, there were a number of confessions but these were from local nutcases and were quickly dismissed by the police.

Mothers began accompanying their children on the school run and rumours grew that the killer was a local man.

Unbeknown to the public, the police had been aware of stalkers in the area for some time prior to Pamela's murder. Many women and children had been accosted in and around Elm Park and pupils at Suttons Primary School, in Suttons Avenue in nearby Hornchurch, had found letters on the way to school offering money if they would meet the writer in an out of the way spot.

Police intensified their search for Pamela's missing clothing and on 21 January, two days after the discovery of her body, Pamela's wellingtons were discovered in a ditch in Abbs Cross Lane, three-quarters of a mile from Morecambe Close. The boots were in a paper bag marked 'Leonard's', which reinforced the theory that the killer was a local man.

An inquest opened on 22 January 1939 at Romford, led by Mr

L F Beccles, the local coroner. Chief Inspector Walter Bridger of Scotland Yard asked for an adjournment. Provisionally adjourning the inquest until 4 March, Mr Beccles said, 'I am not in a position to say whether I shall complete the inquest or not'.

The police began to turn their attention to Coronation Drive, remembering Pamela's mention of the road. Some of her friends recalled her chatting to a man in that road.

The police searched door to door along Coronation Drive and even questioned the local milkman, Walter Gynn. Mr Gynn told the police about Leonard Richardson, a 28-year-old married man with a young son.

On 9 January 1939 Ivy Richardson, his pregnant wife, had been admitted to hospital to give birth to their second child, a daughter. Mrs Richardson was discharged on 22 January. In the thirteen days she was in hospital her sister looked after their three-and-a-half year-old son, and another sister, Lilian Gray,

Coronation Drive in Elm Park. Pamela walked to school along it and Leonard Richardson, the chief suspect in her murder, lived on it. Paul Donnelley

came in to clean the house and cook meals for Richardson. He used the time to do some decorating.

Richardson worked shifts at the May and Baker chemical factory on Rainham Road South in Dagenham, near Dagenham East tube station, one stop from Elm Park. (In 1935 May and Baker revolutionised the production of antibiotics with the synthetic sulfa-drug known as M&B693. The May and Baker plant is now owned and run by Sanofi-Aventis.) In the week that started on 9 January Richardson began work at 6 am and finished at 3 pm. Mr Gynn called on him at 5 am as he delivered the milk but the following week Richardson was on the 2-11 pm rota so asked the milkman not to knock for him.

At 1.15 pm on 18 January, Mr Gynn saw Richardson cycling down South End Road away from Coronation Drive. He acknowledged the milkman as he cycled past but then when Richardson reached Wood Lane he stopped and cycled back to Coronation Drive.

The next day Mr Gynn was about his rounds when he saw a light in the Richardsons' kitchen at 5.20 am.

Pamela Coventry was buried in Barking Cemetery on 26 January and 2,500 lined the streets of Elm Park to watch the cortege pass and a further 5,000 went to the cemetery to view the interment.

It was on the day of Pamela's funeral that the police first questioned Leonard Richardson. During questioning he rolled a cigarette from his tobacco pouch and began to smoke. Richardson had the habit of keeping his fag butts to make new cigarettes. His pouch held fourteen butts. Police confiscated the tobacco and the butts and sent it for analysis to a chemist who worked for the Imperial Tobacco Company in Bristol.

In his interview Richardson told police that he had been resident in Coronation Drive for about three years and so was *au fait* with Elm Park. He would set off for his 2 pm shift at work at about 1.25 pm and cycle to Rainham Road South.

On Monday, 16 January, a still at May and Baker bubbled over and the fumes hurt Richardson's eyes and throat. However, the accident was not serious enough for him to be sent home early and he cycled home, arriving at 11.20 pm. That night Richardson stayed up until 3 am painting his kitchen.

The next day, he told police, he could not remember how he went to work but was definite that on the Wednesday he had travelled by train, the one stop on the District Line to Dagenham East and then walked the five minutes to the factory.

That day Richardson rose at 9.30 am and continued the painting. His sister-in-law arrived to cook for him and she left some time between 1 pm and 1.30 pm. Richardson, so he told the police, was not feeling well and considered taking the day off. He soldiered in, leaving home at 1.40 pm and arrived at work at 1.55 pm.

Richardson sought out the foreman and told him he felt unwell due to the fumes accident and was sent home. He got back to Coronation Drive at 3 pm. He went straight to bed and stayed there for two hours.

At 5 pm he rose and cycled to The Broadway to buy some putty before going to see George Alexander Steen, his GP, at Sark, in Abbs Cross Lane complaining of stinging eyes. He was treated for conjunctivitis. When he got home he went back to the kitchen decorating before retiring at midnight.

The police asked Richardson if he had spoken to any children and asked them to run errands. He said he did ask one small girl but she ran away. There were small cuts on the fingers of Richardson's hands.

The police thoroughly checked Richardson's story: his doctor confirmed that he had visited; the factory corroborated his arrival time at work; and a neighbour said that he had indeed seen Richardson approach a girl but she had ran away.

On 28 January a schoolboy found a parcel wrapped in the *News Chronicle* of 11 January as he crossed Elm Park Railway Bridge. The parcel bound by insulating tape contained a yellow badge, two metal buttons and a section of black cable that was identical to that used to truss Pamela Coventry.

The boy took his find to the police and Mrs Coventry

The Broadway in Elm Park – on Pamela Coventry's route to school. Paul
Donnelley

identified the buttons and badge as belonging to Pamela.

Police obtained a search warrant and raided Leonard
Richardson's house, which was 450 steps away from the ditch in
which Pamela's body was found. The findings were
disappointing – a run of copies of the *News Chronicle* from 4-12
January with the edition dated 11 January missing, some tarred
string, insulating tape and a raincoat with some bloodspots on
it. It was certainly not enough to hold Richardson for further
questioning.

A few days later, the police received a visit from a Mr Curley,
a neighbour of Leonard Richardson. Mr Curley had said that
Richardson had confided in him worries that the fumes at the

factory were making him sexually excited and with his wife pregnant he had no outlet for these feelings. The previous month he had handed Mr Curley a length of creosoted string attached to green cable.

On 1 February, police called at May and Baker and arrested Leonard Richardson, and in the early hours of 2 February they charged him with the murder of Pamela Coventry.

On 24 February, the Crown presented its case. Prosecuting counsel Mr Parham said, 'There had been sexual interference with both organs', but the evidence against Richardson consisted of the cable, the newspaper and the cigarette butt. It was not the strongest case ever put before a court of law.

On 10 March, Home Office chemist Dr Roche Lynch, who had examined the creosoted string given to the police by Mr Curley, said it was similar to that found on Pamela Coventry's body. Dr Roche added that the insulating tape found in Richardson's shed was of the same kind as that used to wrap the parcel found by the schoolboy. He also had found a dozen blood spots on Richardson's raincoat and smears on his inside right trouser pocket. Although the blood on the trousers was human it was not possible to identify it.

Expert Mr Jollyman examined the cigarette butt found with Pamela's body and those in Richardson's tobacco pouch. He said that the tobacco and papers were all of a common enough brand, used by hundreds of thousands of smokers. He pointed out that there were sixty million cigarette papers of that make in circulation at any one time. However, the way the cigarette paper was folded was unusual. There was an underturn or reverse fold at one end of the paper.

On 27 March 1939, the murder trial of Leonard Richardson opened at the Old Bailey. Leading the case for the Crown was Laurence Austin Byrne (born 1896, died 1965) and Mr G Howard, while Roger Winn and Hixon Brown represented the defendant.

The milkman Walter Gynn gave evidence and stuck to his belief that the date he had seen the light in Richardson's kitchen was 18 January. Counsel suggested that the date was either the ninth or nineteenth but My Gynn was adamant.

Lilian Gray took the stand and she said that while at the Richardsons' she had used a copy of the *News Chronicle* to light a fire.

Sir Bernard Spilsbury appeared in the witness box. *The Oxford Dictionary of National Biography* declares, 'When Spilsbury was at the peak of his professional influence during the 1910s to the 1930s, his opinion was virtually unquestioned among many jurors'. The defence suggested that the bloodspots could have come from a previous accident that had caused the cuts on the knuckles, but Sir Bernard was adamant. The bloodspots could not have occurred in that fashion and came, he said, from Pamela's nose as she was being strangled by the accused.

Dr Roche Lynch testified that the bloodspots 'definitely could not be explained by the injury to the finger[s]'.

Mr Jollyman said that around half of the cigarette papers used in the country were the same make as that used by Leonard Richardson.

The defence counsel Roger Winn produced an envelope that contained eighteen cigarette butts collected from a working men's club. Eleven were found to be of the same paper as that smoked by Leonard Richardson. Mr Winn asked the judge, Sir Anthony Hawke, to halt the trial through lack of evidence. Mr Justice Hawke replied that only the jury could stop the proceedings so Leonard Richardson took the stand on 29 March.

He was confident and composed in the witness box and said that the milkman had been confused by the dates and that if a light had been on in his house it had been left on by mistake.

The cuts on his hands he explained away by saying that he had hurt himself at work.

The Richardson family gave evidence next. They were completely convinced of his innocence and it was Ivy Richardson whose idea it was to collect the cigarette butts to compare with the one found on Pamela's body. She and her

Leonard Richardson was tried at the Old Bailey for the murder of Pamela Coventry.

brother had collected a large number and persuaded Frank Hall, the general manager of the Rizla Cigarette Paper Company to examine them. Mr Hall stated that many people used the underturn to roll their own and it was not a particularly unusual trait.

Violet Cavalier, a neighbour of the Richardsons, told the court that she had shared a train carriage with him on the Tuesday.

By lunchtime on the fifth day, 31 March, the jury had heard enough and when they returned to their seats they passed a note to Mr Justice Hawke saying that they did not need to listen to closing arguments from counsel or his summing up because there was insufficient evidence for the case to proceed.

The judge formally acquitted Richardson and told him he was free to go. Outside the Old Bailey the jury lined up to shake hands with him and to wish him well. The foreman said, 'As foreman of the jury, let me congratulate you. All the best, Richardson'.

Leonard Richardson had received many letters of support while on remand in prison from friends, neighbours and colleagues urging him not to give up. May and Baker had kept his job open for him and continued to pay his wages while he was incarcerated.

The murderer of Pamela Coventry remains unknown.

Chapter 13

The Rayleigh Bathchair Murder

'My father is now out of his suffering, and I earnestly hope that my mother will now have a more happy and normal life'

n 1 September 1939 Germany invaded Poland and set in wheels the motion that would lead to the Second World War and the deaths of more than sixty million people.

Air raids over England were commonplace by 1940 and so residents in Essex were used to the drone of German bombers overhead, especially those who lived near Hornchurch airfield and other militarily strategic areas.

People living in and around Hockley Road in Rayleigh had become inured to German bombs falling on their homes. They were used to the sirens going off to warn them of an impending raid but the afternoon of Friday, 23 July 1943 was different. There were no sirens but, around lunchtime, there was a large explosion about a half mile from the town centre, near a house called Gattens.

Enemy action was discounted but a morass of metal and flesh lay close by. A man's left leg was hanging from a tree fifteen feet above the ground, thirty feet away, while the right leg was forty-eight feet away in a front garden. The man was obviously dead and nearby lay a woman screaming in pain, with blood pouring down her legs. The man's torso was some yards behind her.

The explosion had blown out the windows of nearby houses. Neighbours came out to help and some administered first aid to the woman who had shrapnel wounds to her legs. She was taken to Southend Municipal Hospital.

It was in quiet Hockley Road in Rayleigh that a brutal murder occurred.
Essex Police Museum

The first editions of the local newspaper, the *Southend-on-Sea and County Pictorial*, reported that the man had been killed by a bomb dropped from a low-flying German aeroplane.

The next day, an autopsy was carried out by a Dr Gilmour at the Southend Municipal Hospital and he concluded that the explosion had come from below the victim, not from above him. The man had not been killed by a German but had been murdered. Forensic examination showed that a British anti-tank mine, known as the Hawkins Grenade Number 75, had caused the explosion. The metal fragments were discovered to be the remnants of a wheelchair and the injured woman was Elsie Irene

Mitchell, forty-six, of 12, Hillview Road, Rayleigh. She was one of three nurses hired to care for a forty-seven-year-old invalid businessman called Archibald Brown. He lived at Summerfield, 19, London Hill in Rayleigh and his family owned the mill T J Brown & Son which had opened in 1809 and was sail-operated until 1906, when oil was used to power it.

The first policeman to investigate was Chief Inspector Draper who then passed the case on to Superintendent George H Totterdell, the head of Essex CID, who was on leave but was recalled to take charge of the case.

Archibald Brown was born in Rayleigh in 1896, the son of Thomas James Brown, and saw three years' service in the Great War. In 1920 he was involved in a motorcycle accident and gradually his spine became paralysed, finally losing the use of his legs in 1938. In the summer of 1922 he married Dorothy Lucy Willans. In October 1923 their elder son, Eric James, was born. A younger boy, Colin, was born in 1927. In 1929 Thomas James Brown died leaving his son £20,405 (£803,684 at 2004 values). The subsequent years had not been kind to Archibald Brown and by 1943 he was bitter, in constant pain and reliant on a wheelchair. He did, however, possess a cruel streak and kept his wife and sons on a very short leash. He summoned his wife by ringing a bell, and would not allow her to visit her mother in nearby Rochford. He often hit his elder son. In July 1943 Eric was home on compassionate leave from service with the Suffolk Regiment. His mother had written to the commanding officer on 17 May 1943 asking if Eric could be relieved duty because of his father's worsening health. In the Army Eric had been trained to use Hawkins Grenades Number 75, which were intended to blow the tracks from tanks.

The police believed that the grenade had been fixed to the bottom of Archibald Brown's wheelchair and thought it a miracle that Mrs Mitchell had not been killed as well as her master. The velveteen cushions and frame of the chair had saved her from more serious injuries.

When she was well enough, she told the police that the

wheelchair was usually kept in the Anderson shelter and at 1.45 pm, when she had gone to get it, she discovered the door to the shelter was locked from the inside. She went to see Mrs Brown to inform her and as the two women made their way back they bumped into a flustered Eric who was leaving. He was angry and tried to avoid answering their questions as to why the shelter door was locked. The two women pushed the chair into the house and helped Archibald Brown in. He was dressed in pyjamas and a dressing gown and they placed a plaid travelling rug over his legs. They put two pillows behind him and wrapped a rug around him.

They set off and were about a mile down the Hockley Road when Archibald Brown decided that he wanted a cigarette and reached into his dressing gown pocket. Mrs Mitchell stopped the chair and walked round to the front to light the cigarette and then returned to behind the chair. Before she had gone half a dozen paces the chair exploded.

The police spent five hours questioning Brown's widow and discovered that he had taken a liking to his nurse, although Mrs Brown stressed that there was no impropriety in their relationship.

The mother said that the relationship between father and elder son was strained. The younger boy, Colin, was studying accountancy in Southend and was said to have a good relationship with his father. Eric was different. He was something of an oddball. He suffered from mood swings and was difficult to have at home so he was removed from his school at Rayleigh and sent to a boarding school near Walthamstow. On leaving school in 1940 he worked as a junior clerk at Barclays Bank in Rochford. Two years later, in June 1942, he was asked to leave after the manager became annoyed with Brown's odd behaviour.

On 1 October 1942, Eric Brown received his call-up papers and joined the Army in the 8th Battalion of the Suffolk Regiment, and was posted to Spilsby in Lincolnshire. At the camp was a store of 175 Hawkins Grenades, 144 of them were

Eric Brown planted a bomb under this bathchair to kill his tyrannical father.
Essex Police Museum

primed and in working order. The Hawkins Grenade was about seven inches by four inches and resembled a large bicycle lamp. On 21 April 1943, Eric had attended a lecture specifically about the Hawkins Grenade mine.

The police investigated the remnants of the bathchair and noted that the pressure plate had been adapted to set off the explosive device. It would usually take the weight of a tank to set off the device and Archibald Brown was obviously considerably lighter.

On 20 August, Eric Brown was taken in for questioning under caution at Rayleigh police station by Superintendent George H Totterdell, accompanied by Detective Chief Inspector Draper and Detective Inspector Jack 'Trapper' Barkway. It did not take the three experienced policeman long to wheedle a confession out of the young soldier. He explained that he had killed his father to save his mother.

> *I want to tell you the whole story. For this last four and half years, and even before that, life has ceased to exist for my mother, but has become a complete drudgery as a result of my father's treatment to her. I decided that the only real way in which my mother could lead a normal life, and my father to be released from his sufferings, was for him to die mercifully. I therefore decided to cause his death in a manner which would leave him no longer in suffering. This was only decided upon a matter of days before his death. After nearly a fortnight of seeing just exactly what my mother was forced to endure, I realised that this could not be allowed to go on. Primarily for my mother's sake, but also, to a lesser degree, for my father's sake, I placed the grenade under my father's chair, not realising at the time that, although it would kill him, just what his death would mean to me and all those near him. My father is now out of his suffering, and I earnestly hope that my mother will now have a more happy and normal life. This I declare is the only motive I had for bringing about my father's death. His death was, in truth, a great shock to me, but what I did I am not afraid to answer for.*

Eric Brown said that he had stolen the device from the army and used his interest in gadgets to alter the pressure needed to set off the grenade. He was arrested and formally charged with murder.

On Monday, 20 September 1943, Eric appeared at Southend County Petty Sessions. Mr J P Nolan defended him while Mr J F Claxton appeared for the Crown. Called to give evidence, Mrs Brown revealed the extent of her husband's bullying of her and their elder son. He would throw hot tea at her and on one occasion attempted to strangle her. When Detective Inspector Barkway gave evidence he referred to Eric's confession, only for Mr Nolan to suggest that Detective Inspector Barkway and Detective Chief Inspector Draper had told Eric Brown that, unless he confessed, they would make things difficult for his mother. They said that they knew that she was the prime mover in the murder and that Eric was merely following her instructions. Both men vigorously denied the accusation. Eric was committed for trial at Essex Assizes.

The murder trial began on 4 November of the same year before Judge Atkinson at Shire Hall, Chelmsford. The courtroom was packed with spectators. Prosecuting was Sir Charles Doughty, KC, assisted by Mr J C Llewellyn. Cecil Havers, KC, and Wilfrid Fordham represented Eric who pleaded not guilty. His defence consisted of suggesting that he was not in his right mind, having been driven to act by his father's unreasonable behaviour. One specialist, Dr Rowland Hill, called by the defence diagnosed Eric Brown as 'a typical schizophrenic'. He added:

He came to the prison in a happy buoyant frame of mind… he suddenly realised for the first time that by what he had done people might call him a murderer.

The prison doctor, R G Lyster, gave his opinion that Brown was sane, but reported that, whilst in custody, he had attempted to commit suicide on 25 October by cutting his throat.

The jury found Eric brown guilty but insane after forty-five minutes of deliberation. Mr Justice Atkinson ordered Eric Brown to be detained in an asylum during His Majesty's pleasure.

There remains an oddity in the case. Eric Brown altered the pressure needed for the 75 Hawkins Grenade to explode so why did it not go off immediately his father sat in the bathchair at the house, Summerfield? Also, did Eric Brown not think that perhaps Nurse Mitchell or indeed even his mother might have been killed by the explosion as well, had it gone off at home? In addition, if the nurse had on a whim changed the route and taken Archibald Brown right into the High Street the casualties could have been in the dozens.

Elsie Irene Mitchell was left with a limp and an injury to her arm but resumed nursing when she had recuperated.

Archibald Brown was buried a week after his murder on 30 July 1943.

Rayleigh Mill is now no longer an active mill. The sails that were removed in 1906 have been restored and the building is now home to a museum.

Eric Brown was released in 1975, having spent thirty-two years in an asylum. He was only fifty-one years old.

Detective Inspector Jack 'Trapper' Barkway later became the head of Essex CID.

Chapter 14

The Body in the Marshes

'he found the torso of a man,
minus the head and legs'

Brian Donald Hume was born in Swanage, Dorset, on 20 December 1919. He was the illegitimate son of a schoolmistress and this affected him throughout his life. He claimed, 'I was born with a chip on my shoulder'.

His mother was unable to raise him and placed him in a West Country orphanage, which he hated and he bore a special loathing for the three old ladies who ran it.

In the orphanage, the children were regarded as 'the product of sin' and treated accordingly. The three old ladies even kept a parrot that shouted 'bastard' to remind the young residents of their status.

The ladies certainly did not spare the rod to spoil the child. Often the children slept eight to a bed and food was in short supply. Hume claimed that they were only given jam on Christmas Day. As punishment, they were often locked in a filthy, dank cellar for hours on end. The old ladies told the children that if they misbehaved they would be taken away by a scary figure known as the Old Green Gypsy. Unbelievably, they got one of the staff to dress as the bogeyman and scare the children.

Hume was locked in the cellar one day with a girl after they were both caught misbehaving. The two children clung to one another terrified that the Old Green Gypsy would visit them. Sure enough the apparition appeared before them but Hume spotted that the shoes of the creature belonged to a member of staff. He was so angry that he had been conned that he chased after them with an axe. He was then just seven years old.

The following year Hume was then adopted by his grandmother and taken away from the home. But far from being a now idyllic childhood, it was just as bad. He was sent to live with his Aunt Doodie, the headmistress of a small Hampshire village school. Doodie turned out to be as cruel and heartless as the old ladies who ran the orphanage. Doodie had two daughters, Peggy and Betty, but seemed to delight in arranging plans for the family and purposely excluding Hume.

One time she sorted out a holiday and Doodie, her husband and the girls went and Hume was left home alone to look after the house and chickens. On one occasion when he was alone he took a shotgun and shot Doodie's favourite cockerel and threw it into the cesspool. On her return, Hume told his aunt that the bird had drowned.

It was against this background that Hume lost all faith in humanity. His situation was to get worse when Doris the maid told him that Doodie was not, in fact his aunt but his mother. This revelation, according to Hume himself, was the catalyst to make him bear a grudge against society even more. She forced him to leave Queen Mary's Grammar School at 14 and get a job in a Farnborough kitchen while keeping up the pretence that she was his aunt.

His ambition was to work on a cruise liner but abandoned this plan after he was given a lift to Hammersmith where a lorry driver befriended him and helped him find somewhere to live and a job.

While in London, fifteen-year-old Hume went to Somerset House where birth, marriage and death certificates were then stored and looked himself up. He was horrified to see that Aunt Doodie was, in fact Mummy Doodie and the space for his father's name was left blank.

Hume was determined to have his revenge on the society that he felt had betrayed him. He began joyriding and petty thieving; he joined the Communist party at seventeen and began a life of fraud. In 1936 he was often in the thick of things during the height of Oswald Mosley's skirmishes. However, it is thought that Hume was involved because he liked a punch-up rather than because of any strongly held anti-Fascist beliefs.

In September 1939, he joined the Royal Air Force but contracted meningitis in 1940 and was declared unfit for duties. He was invalided out in 1941 and quickly returned to his nefarious activities. He sold Finlinson's Old English Gin to nightclubs – it was, in fact, surgical spirits combined with a tiny amount of gin. He even bought an RAF uniform for £5 and called himself Pilot Officer Don Hume, DFM.

He was sent to Feltham Borstal after cashing several hundred pounds worth of forged cheques at RAF stations.

In 1942, Hume began a number of successful companies including a legitimate electrician's business. He also patented the Little Atom Electric Toaster.

However, things began to go wrong and by the end of 1948 Hume was living with his twenty-seven-year-old pregnant wife, Cynthia Wright (they were married at Hendon Register Office on 29 September 1948), in a seven-room maisonette at 620 Finchley Road in Golders Green, north London. He was also short of money.

In early 1949, while doing his dodgy deals, Hume met again Stanley Setty, a flash, nattily dressed forty-six-year-old Jewish spiv and Warren Street car dealer in the Hollywood Club in the West End, near Marble Arch. Setty had been born in Baghdad, Iraq in 1903 as Sulman Seti. His parents moved to England when he was five and as soon as he was old enough Setty began doing deals, not always successfully. In 1928 he was sentenced to fifteen months in prison for twenty-three offences under the Debtors and Bankruptcy Act. By the time he met Hume for the second time he was living in a luxury flat in Maitland Court, Lancaster Gate, with his sister, Eva Ouri, and brother-in-law, Aly Ouri. (The first, brief meeting had occurred in December 1947 when Hume bought a small van for £37 from Setty.)

However, Hume still had an eye for the main chance and he and Setty realised that they could be good for each other.

So began their joint venture. By day Hume would continue to

work as an electrician and at night he worked for Setty stealing cars to order. Setty would use log-books from write-offs and match them to the cars brought to him by Hume.

Hume had also by this time learned to fly a plane and used this skill in his work for Setty. He smuggled anything and everything, including people. It was this sideline, which included forging petrol coupons, that made the earnings from his legitimate electrician's business look pitiful. Hume saw the riches that Setty had accumulated and wanted some for himself.

On Tuesday, 4 October 1949, Hume went out drinking and when he returned to his Golders Green maisonette his wife and eleven-week-old baby daughter Alison were out. Sitting on the sofa in his living room was Stanley Setty. It has never been satisfactorily explained how Setty got into the flat without Mrs Hume being present. They began to argue over Setty's mistreatment of Hume's beloved mongrel, Tony, a few days earlier. Hume pulled out an SS dagger and at 7.35 pm stabbed Setty repeatedly. Hume was to say later, 'I watched the life run from him like water down a drain'.

He put the body in the coalhole and drove Setty's yellow Citroen, registration CJN 444, back to his garage in Cambridge Terrace Mews.

On 5 October, he dismembered Setty in the kitchen with a hacksaw and a lino knife and made three separate packages, one each for the head, legs and torso. Setty had been carrying £1,000 in cash and Hume removed £100 of the least bloodstained notes.

Hume hired a Singer car and put the head and legs into the vehicle and drove to Elstree airport. He got into the two-seater Auster aeroplane belonging to the United Services Flying Club, an aircraft he had used previously for his smuggling activities.

Hume flew over the Channel and threw out the head, legs, SS dagger, the hacksaw and lino knife he had used to cut up Setty.

Bad weather forced Setty to land at Southend Airport. He took a taxi back to London and paid the cabbie with one of the £5 notes he had taken from Setty.

On 6 October he hired Joe Staddon, a decorator, to restain the

Donald Hume used this plane to dump the body of Stanley Setty in the Channel. Essex Police Museum

floor and cover the bloodstains in his home and, with an audacity rarely seen, Hume had Mr Staddon help him carry the parcel containing the remains of Setty down to his car.

Hume again drove to the aerodrome, this time accompanied by his dog and began his flight over the Channel to dump the remnants of Setty. To ensure the parcel sank Hume put lead weights on it. However as with the best laid plans the weights came adrift from the parcel and it floated up the Essex marshes where, on 21 October 1949, Sidney Tiffin, a farm worker, found it in Dengie Marshes near Tillingham.

Opening it he found the torso of a man, minus the head and legs. An examination revealed that the man had been stabbed to death. The corpse was identified as Stanley Setty. Mr Tiffin received a £1,000 reward offered by the Setty family on 14 October 1949 to trace him. The murder had excited the attentions of the press. The *Daily Express* ran a headline: 'Dealer with 200 Fivers Vanishes'.

One of the £5 notes that Setty had had on him came into circulation and was traced by police to a Southend taxi firm. The driver explained that he had taken a man to London for the fare.

Hume was traced and a left luggage ticket was discovered at his home. It was for Golders Green Tube and the locker contained a cabin trunk that had temporarily held Setty's body.

When the police searched Hume's maisonette they found bloodstains under the floorboards of the hall and living room. The police arrested Hume on 27 October and took him to Albany Street police station where he came up with a fanciful story that he had been forced by three thugs, Mac, Greeny and The Boy, at the threat of violence to dispose of three parcels. He did not know what they contained but he was offered £50 for the job and The Boy produced a gun to seal the deal.

Hume appeared before Bow Street Magistrates Court on 26 November 1949, charged with the murder of Stanley Setty.

Pleading not guilty, Hume's trial began at Court No 1 of the Old Bailey on 18 January 1950 before Mr Justice Lewis (who stepped down the next day through ill-health and was replaced by Mr Justice Sellers, who brought in a new jury). Christmas Humphries prosecuted for the Crown and R F Levy, KC, defended Hume.

Hume persisted with his tale of the three hooligans forcing him to dispose of parcels. When questioned about the bloodstains in his front room Hume said that a child might have caused them.

Although the evidence appeared to be stacked up against Hume a glimmer of hope surfaced when Mr Levy asked the pathologist Donald Teare if he was sure Setty 'had been killed by one assailant'. Professor Teare took a full two minutes to answer and then said, 'I think the absence of marks of defence on the body renders it more likely that he was killed by more than one person'. It posed a question. If more than one person had killed Setty, why was Hume standing in the dock alone? The jury failed to reach a verdict on 26 January. A second jury was empanelled and when the Crown offered no evidence they were instructed by the judge to find Hume not guilty of murder. A lesser charge of accessory to murder was introduced and Hume pleaded guilty and was sentenced to twelve years in prison.

Hume was released on 1 February 1958 having spent some time in Dartmoor where he had been nicknamed 'The Fuse' by his fellow cons because of his knowledge of electrics.

Hume changed his name to Donald Brown. In May 1958 he was approached by the *Sunday Pictorial* and for £2,000 (£31,300 at 2005 values) confessed to the murder of Setty during an argument at his home. He admitted making up the villains Mac, Greeny and The Boy in the newspaper in June 1958. Due to the law of double jeopardy it was not possible to retry Hume for Setty's murder.*

On 25 May 1958, under the name John Stephen Bird, Hume flew to Switzerland where he passed himself off as a Canadian test pilot. He spent lavishly the money he earned from the *Pictorial*. He travelled to America and considered robbing a bank when he ran low on funds. At the end of June he returned to Switzerland where he formulated his plan to rob a bank in England.

At 12 pm on 2 August 1958, having taken two pep pills and drunk a half of bitter, he burst into the Midland bank in Boston Manor Road, Brentford. He shot a cashier, Frank Lewis, and stole about £1,500. On 3 August, he flew back to Zurich and continued his amorous pursuit of hairdresser Trudi Sommer (his wife divorced him while he was in prison).

On 12 November, he again robbed the same bank making off with £300 and shot the branch manager. He dashed to Kew Bridge where he caught a train to Waterloo. Adopting his Canadian test pilot persona he travelled back to Zurich.

---

* The law was abondoned after eight hundred years by Tony Blair's government in April 2005. A Home Office spokesman said: 'It is important the public should have full confidence in the ability of the criminal justice system to deliver justice. This can be undermined if it is not possible to convict offenders for very serious crimes where there is strong and viable evidence of their guilt' conveniently forgetting that they would indeed have been convicted if there had been 'strong and viable evidence of their guilt'. On 11 September 2006, William Dunlop became the first person to be convicted of murder after previously being aquitted. He was tried twice for the murder of Julie Hogg in Billingham in 1989, but two juries failed to reach a verdict and he was formally acquitted in 1991. Some years later, he confessed to the crime, and was convicted of perjury.

Hume had left a raincoat on the train and inside was written a name that the police knew to be one of his aliases. They guessed that the bank robber was Donald Hume.

On 30 January 1959, Hume went to the Gewerbe Bank in Zurich and shot a cashier. He only managed to grab a few coins before the alarm was set off. Chased by staff and customers Hume shot Arthur Maag, a fifty-year-old taxi driver, who tried to prevent his escape.

Captured by the police Hume pretended to be a Pole but was caught out when the authorities produced a Polish interpreter. Dr Guggenbuhl-Craig, a Zurich psychiatrist, examined Hume and pronounced him fit to stand trial.

On remand Hume wrote *The Dead Stay Dumb*, a 60,000 word novel about gangsters and their molls.

Tried at Winterthur on 24 September 1959, Hume was found guilty and sentenced to hard labour for life six days later. He served the first three months of his sentence in solitary confinement in Regensdorf Jail.

On 20 August 1976, the Swiss authorities released him. He was flown to Heathrow and examined by two psychiatrists. Donald Hume was sent to Broadmoor, the hospital for the criminally insane.

Brian Donald Hume died in Broadmoor on 19 April 1988.

Chapter 15

The Sleepwalking Murder

*'I found I was over Jean and I had
my hands around her throat'*

During the Second World War it was said of GIs stationed in Britain: 'They're overpaid, oversexed and over here' (to which the Americans responded that the Brits were 'underpaid, undersexed and under Eisenhower'). Although their numbers have decreased there is still a heavy American military presence in the UK and it was greater still during the Cold War.

Great Dunmow has also achieved a measure of fame through the Dunmow Flitch. The Dunmow Flitch Trials exist to award a flitch, or side of bacon, to married couples (who may come from anywhere in the world) if they can satisfy the judge and jury of six maidens and six bachelors that in 'twelve month and a day' they have 'not wished themselves unmarried again'.

The Dunmow Flitch is reported to date back to 1104 and the Augustinian Priory of Little Dunmow, which was founded by Lady Juga Baynard. Reginald Fitzwalter, the Lord of the Manor, and his wife dressed as peasants and asked to be blessed by the prior a

Memorial in Great Dunmow to the American soldiers who served during the Second World War.

Little Dunmow Priory.

year and a day after marriage. The prior, impressed by their devotion, gave them a flitch of bacon. Fitzwalter told them who he really was and gave his land to the priory on the condition a flitch should be awarded to any couple who could claim they were similarly devoted.

By the 14th century the Dunmow Flitch had become well-known enough to be mentioned in books. William Langland who lived on the Welsh borders, mentions it in his 1362 work *The Vision of Piers Plowman*, in a manner that implies his readers will be aware of the tradition.

Chaucer, writing less than half a century later alludes to the Dunmow Flitch Trials in *The Wife of Bath's Tale*.

However, it was not until 1445 that the winners of the Flitch were officially recorded. The earliest record of a successful claimant to the Dunmow Flitch is Richard Wright who travelled from Norwich to try and take home the bacon. The win is recorded in documents from the Priory of Little Dunmow held by the British Museum.

On New Year's Eve 1960, a Sunday, Jean Sylvia Constable, aged twenty, left her home in Abels Road, Halstead, and announced that she was going to a party in London. Jean, who worked in a local plastics factory, was somewhat starry-eyed when it came to the glamorous American service personnel. She spent most of her spare time in pubs she knew they would frequent and her favourite GI was Staff Sergeant Willis Eugene Boshears, twenty-nine and a married father of three, from Michigan. Boshears was a member of the darts team at his local the *Kicking Donkey*, where he was known as Little Mac because of his diminutive size. He had flown twenty-nine combat missions over Korea and won the US Air Medal three times. In 1954 he had married a woman from Ayr, also called Jean. They had two daughters, both born in America, and a son, George, who was born on 11 December 1960 in Scotland. Jean Boshears had specifically gone to Scotland for the child's birth.

On that cold last day of 1960 Staff Sergeant Boshears got up at 6.15 am and, after collecting his pay, went for breakfast in the NCO's club at the American fighter plane base at RAF Wethersfield where he served in the 20th Field Maintenance Squadron. His breakfast consisted of two vodkas and two vodka chasers and an egg. Boshears had recently had some teeth out so could not manage too much food. The rest of the morning, he spent downing drinks before leaving the base with a large bottle of 100 per cent proof vodka in his hands. He headed back to his flat which was in a large house in The Close, Great Dunmow, CM6 1EW, but stopped off for a couple of beers at

Great Dunmow High Street, an area once occupied by the parish workhouse.

Great Bardfield. At home, he downed a large vodka and lemonade before heading out the door to Billericay where he went into *The Bell Hotel, The Boar* and then *The Bell* again. At *The Bell*, he fell into conversation with Jean Constable and David Sault, also twenty, and an apprentice engineer from Leicester, at 11.30 pm. They had met in *The Boar's Head* before moving onto the pub in which they met Boshears.

At closing time, they repaired to Staff Sergeant Boshears's flat, ten miles away, by taxi. They continued drinking and chatting, and Boshears turned on his record player. At some point that night, another American serviceman came down and told them to turn down the music. When Staff Sergeant Boshears left the room, Jean Constable and David Sault began to have sex and continued when the GI came back. Staff Sergeant Boshears showed them around the flat and when they got to the bedroom the twenty-year-olds had sex again.

Staff Sergeant Boshears dragged a mattress in front of the fire and when Constable and Sault had finished their canoodling, he suggested they have some more to drink. Jean undressed in front of both men and then they all went to sleep on the mattress.

At 12.45 am, David Sault awoke and got dressed. He shook the staff sergeant awake and asked him where the nearest taxi rank was. He left the flat and Boshears fell back asleep next to a heavily slumbering Jean Constable.

Staff-Sergeant Boshears later recalled:

> *I went to sleep almost immediately. The next thing I remembered is that I felt something pulling at my mouth. I was not awake but this woke me up, and I found I was over Jean and I had my hands around her throat. Jean was dead, and I panicked. I started to cut her hair off. Then I took the body to the spare room and left it. I dressed her in the way in which she was later found. I took the sheets and blankets off the bed and put them in the bathtub to soak and went in and went to sleep.*

The next day, 2 January 1961, at 11.30pm Mr Boshears disposed of the partially clothed body under a mulberry bush in a lay-by at Oaken Hill, on the A604 Halstead-Hedingham road, just outside Ridgewell. It lay there until it was discovered by lorry driver Sidney Ambrose on 3 January who was desperate to relieve himself and was looking for a suitable venue.

The autopsy was carried out by Professor Francis Camps, one of the so-called 'Three Musketeers' of eminent pathologists of the time – the other two being Professor Keith Simpson and Professor Donald Teare.

Detetctive Chief Superintendent Ernest 'Jack' Barkway, the head of Essex Police CID, led the case assisted by Detective Inspector Len Jeavons, who was acquainted with most, if not all, of the local villains.

The arms and motto of Great Dunmow.

When the police learned that the victim liked associating with GIs they moved a step nearer to solving the case.

Staff-Sergeant Boshears was arrested on 4 January and taken to Castle Hedingham police station where he was charged with Jean Constable's murder. He was taken to Brixton prison that night and the next morning taken back to Castle Hedingham to appear before magistrates. Major Carl B Prestin of the United States Judge Advocate's Department asked for Boshears to be turned over to them for a court martial, but the police objected and Sir Theobald Mathew, the Director of Public Prosecutions, supported their application. Boshears was remanded in custody until 13 January.

His trial began at Essex Assizes in Chelmsford on 4 February 1961. He pleaded not guilty, claiming that, since he had killed Jean Constable in his sleep, no crime had been committed. Mr Justice Glyn-Jones, the judge, and the prosecuting counsel,

Stanley Rees, QC, were distrustful of this defence, put forward in court by Gerald Hines, defending. Sharing the view of the judge and prosecuting counsel was Professor Francis Camps.

He testified that the airman would have applied pressure for thirty seconds and that 'Boshears would probably have felt the girl moving, even if he was half asleep.'

Mr Hines questioned the length of time that Professor Camps said would have been necessary for death to follow and the pathologist admitted that his findings were a matter of conjecture.

The judge questioned him: 'He could not possibly have carried this through without waking up?', to which Camps responded:

I should think that it is certainly within the bounds of improbability. My reason, from my findings, is this process would take a certain amount of time, and during that period the person would go through certain phases of movement, and from the description given of finding her suddenly dead like that I don't think it fits in with that type of death.

When it was his turn to testify the court became hushed and waited to hear what the American had to say. Boshears spoke in a low, steady voice.

I sat down on the edge of the mattress next to the sleeping girl. The next thing I remember was I felt something pulling at my mouth. I was not awake when I first felt it. It seemed to wake me up, I was over Jean and had my hands around her throat.

Jean was dead. I panicked. I started to cut her hair off. Then I took her body to the spare room and left it. I dressed her in the way in which she was later found. I took the sheets and the blankets off the bed and out them in the bathtub to soak and went in and went to sleep.

I had no idea of time. When I woke I decided it had been a dream. But when I found the body I was scared and shocked.

I told lies to the police in the first instance because I was scared.

Questioned by his lawyer, Boshears said that he had had no argument with the dead girl, had not wanted to have sex with her and had certainly not wanted to kill her.

At his twenty-two minute summation, Mr Justice Glyn-Jones said:

> *Have you ever heard of a man strangling a woman while he was sound asleep? We have no medical evidence that there exists any record in all the records of the medical profession that such a thing ever happened... You use your common sense and decide whether it happened.*

Intending to be fair, Mr Justice Glyn-Jones told the jury that if Staff Sergeant Boshears had been asleep and committed the murder involuntarily, they should acquit. There were, he informed them, only two verdicts that they could return – guilty of murder, or not guilty of anything. There was no lesser charge of manslaughter.

The jury deliberated for one hour and fifty minutes before they returned and declared Boshears not guilty. There were shouts from the public gallery after the foreman read out the verdict.

Gerald Hines rose to his feet and asked the judge if his client could be released. A still surprised Mr Justice Glyn-Jones agreed.

Boshears later said:

> *It has been six weeks of hell. I'm still in a daze. I cannot believe it's true that I am a free man. British justice? It's wonderful. My wife has forgiven me. She came to see me in prison while I was awaiting trial to tell me so. I am longing to see my kids again. I kept a picture of them in my cell.*

There would be no happy ending.

In March 1961, Willis Eugene Boshears was quietly transferred back to an American base in Glasgow, Montana. He received the $800 back pay that had been withheld while he was in custody.

Four months later in July 1961 Boshears was dismissed from the army. The official statement said that his discharge was 'under other than honourable conditions'.

He was later killed in a car crash.

A week after Boshears was acquitted, another man murdered a woman by stabbing her, then claimed he had been asleep. This time the jury did not believe his story and he was sentenced to life imprisonment.

Chapter 16

Murder Shorts

'Samuel Law had suffered more than a hundred
deep cuts to the face and neck and baby Alfred
had been killed with a hammer.'

Footpad Meets his Match

On 12 September 1690 the Essex highwayman Frank Osborne was hanged at Tyburn (now the site of Marble Arch). Osborne was born at Colchester in 1661 to wealthy parents and became an apprentice goldsmith, later running his own business. Osborne began gambling and soon racked up large debts that he was unable to meet. He did not want to be sent to debtors' prison so he decided to steal the money he owed. He and a comrade robbed the coach of the Earl of Albemarle on the Harwich-Manningtree road despite the nobleman's armed bodyguards. The earl lost 130 guineas, his gold watch and all his jewellery. With some other footpads, Osborne attempted to rob a coach on Hounslow Heath but the armed outriders outshot them and Osborne surrendered. He was taken to Newgate before meeting his fate at Tyburn. He was twenty-nine years old.

Fourteen-year-old Hanged

John Houghton had not yet celebrated his fourteenth birthday in 1810, when he was working as a tap and post boy for a Mr Chinnery at Abridge. One day Mr Chinnery woke up and found that Houghton had gone without so much as saying goodbye. Suspecting that all might not be well, he went to the box where he kept his savings. The box was empty. Mr Chinnery went to the police to report the theft and Houghton was arrested at his mother's house. Houghton confessed to the robbery but said that it had been at the instigation of another servant. The jury did not show mercy and found him guilty. John Houghton was hanged in the third week of March 1810.

I Was a Teenage Arsonist

James Cook was sixteen years old and worked as a cowhand on the farm of William Green in Witham. In 1829 he set a fire that scorched the farm buildings. Taken to court he was charged with arson and found guilty. On 27 March 1829, he was hanged at Springfield Prison, Chelmsford.

Waistcoat Saves Copper

Patrolling his beat in Essex on 4 April 1851, PC Samuel Druce came across two men breaking into a shop. As he attempted an arrest, he was attacked with a knife but the blade failed to penetrate his chest. PC Druce was wearing a very thick waistcoat under his uniform which saved his life. The two men left a false hand in a glove behind and police soon arrested a one-handed poacher called Holden.

Green-eyed Monster Wrecks Lives

Charles Finch suffered from jealousy. The insecurity caused problems in his relationship with his girlfriend. They lived together in London but one day, without telling her, he got up and joined the Land Transport Corps in the Crimea. When he returned, he looked up his belle and found her in her home town of Kelvedon. She agreed to go out with him again, but again the green-eyed monster raised its ugly head and they argued constantly. He walked out on her again. A week later, as she was walking to church, he jumped out on her and slit her throat with a razor. At his trial he pleaded guilty and was sentenced to death. He ate a full breakfast and was executed by William Calcraft on 30 July 1851 at Springfield Prison, Chelmsford. Calcraft was his usual incompetent self and Finch 'struggled violently for some minutes before he died'.

Devils on the Stairs in Clavering

It was the wee small hours of the morning on 14 January 1862 when a blood-soaked twenty-four-year-old called Rebecca Law banged on her mother's door. With her was her six-year-old son. Law confessed to her mother that she had just murdered her husband, Samuel, twenty-seven, and sixteen-week-old baby Alfred. When police arrived at the Laws' cottage, they found Samuel Law had suffered more than a hundred deep cuts to his face and neck and baby Alfred had been killed with a hammer. When she came to trial Law said, 'All the time I was hitting [Samuel] there was a noise on the stairs. They kept blundering up the stairs – I mean the devils – but I wasn't afraid'. Law was diagnosed as a 'melancholic' and 'religiomaniac' although today she would probably be regarded as suffering from post-natal depression. She was found not guilty by reason of insanity and sent to a lunatic asylum.

Homicidal Theft
On 8 February 1871, twenty-eight-year-old Michael Campbell, a Berwick-born tailor and ex-soldier, and three friends broke into a house belonging to forty-nine-year-old Samuel Galloway in Canon Street, Stratford, with intent to burgle. Unfortunately, they were disturbed by Mr Galloway who chased the thieves. As he stood at the edge of his property, they set about him, and as two held his arms another hit him over the head. Ten days later, Mr Galloway died from his injuries. Mrs Galloway had witnessed the assault and duly identified Campbell. At his trial he pleaded guilty to burglary but claimed he had meant no harm to Mr Galloway. William Calcraft hanged Campbell on 24 April 1871 at Springfield Prison, Chelmsford. His was the first 'private' execution in Essex.

Cop Killer Unknown
At 7.40 pm on 4 January 1894, Sergeant John Harvey, whose wife was pregnant with their fourth child, and some colleagues were about their business in Ardleigh when he suddenly disappeared. The next morning his body was found in a snow-covered well of a cottage. Sergeant Harvey's watch had stopped at 8.21 pm and he had injuries to his face. His murder remains unsolved.

Child-killer on the Loose

In January 1899, Jenny Voller was murdered and her body thrown into Loxford Brook in Barking. Mrs Voller had sent five-year-old Jenny to the shops on Harpour Road to buy a pennyworth of linseed. The mother raised the alarm when Jenny failed to return. Both parents went to the shop but Jenny had never arrived, nor had she been seen in any of the other shops on the parade. When her body was found, it had been cut with scissors and the small amount of money in her pockets was missing. The murderer of Jenny Voller was never found.

Suicide-Murder Horror in Southchurch

George Facer and Jeannie Tait set up home together in 1886. Although they never married, they had two children. In early 1900 things began to go wrong and they separated, placing their children with Dr Barnardo's. Jeannie Tait moved to Honiton Road in Southend but stayed in touch with her boyfriend. Facer was keen to effect reconciliation 'for the sake of our children' and so, on 25 June 1901, she agreed to meet him at her home in Southend. It did not go well and they began to argue. Then Facer pulled out a gun and shot his girlfriend twice at point blank range. He then put the pistol to his own head and pulled the trigger. Nothing happened. He fired into the air and again put the gun to his head but the weapon would not fire. He ran off to woods near Thorpe Hall, Southchurch, where he finally succeeded in killing himself. The coroner returned a verdict of murder and suicide while the balance of the mind was disturbed.

Soldier Kills Ex

Bernard White, then nineteen, began dating Maude Garrett, an eighteen-year-old single girl living at Brentwood with her father, in 1901. He was a soldier with the 2nd Battalion of the Essex Regiment but, six weeks into the relationship, he was posted to South Africa to fight in the Boer War. On his return he was shocked to find that his girlfriend had become engaged to not only another man but to another soldier – a Private Jones of the Royal Army Medical Corps.

On 21 May 1903, Maud went to visit her beau in hospital in Warley. While there, she saw White who was with two friends. The three made a discreet exit but his friends were later to say that there seemed an amity between Maude and White. Indeed he told them that she had agreed to meet him the next night. On 22 May, the three went out drinking and left the pub at 9.15 pm. Two of the squaddies went back to their barracks and White met up with Maud as arranged. White had to 'book in' at his camp in Little Warley, near Brentwood, but at around 10.15 pm he crept out again. He was back in his billet by 11 pm. At 5 am the mutilated body of Maud Garrett was discovered at The Gap, a lonely spot near the camp, by a labourer on his way to work. White told his Regimental Sergeant Major that he had been with the dead girl the night she died but claimed she was alive and well when her left her at the barracks' gate. When Superintendent Aldred Marden of Essex Police questioned White, he found blood on the soldier's socks, boots, trousers and cane. Tried on 12-13 November 1903 before Mr Justice Lawrance, White was found guilty and on 1 December 1903, aged twenty-one, he was hanged at Springfield Prison, Chelmsford, by William Billington, assisted by Henry Pierrepoint. One odd fact remains. At about 10.45 pm on the night of the murder Colour Sergeant Harry Roberts on his way back to camp saw a man in civilian clothes about fifty yards from where Maud's body was found. The mystery man was never traced.

Lovers' Quarrel Ends in Murder

Charles Howell, a thirty-year-old soldier in the Suffolk Regiment, was stationed in Colchester. He was dating a nineteen-year-old local girl called Maud Luen. On Whit Monday, 1 June, 1903 the couple went for a walk but were heard arguing at around 9 pm. She said, 'No, I will not go there. It's no use'. He returned to his barracks and said to a fellow squaddie, 'She will not be alive in the morning'. At 9.40 pm the same evening, they met up again, although this time Maud was with her friend, Mrs Tredger, in a lane close to the barracks. He asked for her forgiveness for upsetting her and Maud agreed but just then wanted to be left alone. He put his arm around her and asked for a kiss. Before Maud could reply Howell pulled out a cutthroat razor and cut her throat so deeply that she died almost immediately. Mrs Tredger saw a sergeant from the Suffolks cycling to the barracks and told him what had happened. He apprehended Howell and later handed him to the police who charged him with murder. At his trial, which opened before Mr Justice Wright on 19 June at Chelmsford, Howell's defence team claimed that he was insane and suffering from post-traumatic stress caused by his time in the Boer War. In his closing speech Mr Justice Wright told the jury that they had to be satisfied that he was of sound mind before convicting. The twelve good men and true did convict but recommended that Howell was examined for psychiatric problems. The Home Secretary, Aretas Akers-Douglas, saw no reason to commute the sentence and Howell was hanged at Springfield Prison, Chelmsford, on 7 July by William Billington assisted by John Ellis.

Killed by Accident

On 18 February 1939, twenty-six-year-old George Butterworth confessed at Colchester police station to the murder of his wife, Phyllis, twenty-one. The couple had separated and she had found herself a new beau. Nevertheless, he wanted her back and was regularly calling. On the fateful day they enjoyed a day out at Copford but on the way home she had mentioned the name of her fancy man and in a fit of temper George Butterworth beat her to death with the butt of a .22 Webley pistol. He pushed her body onto the back seat and drove to Colchester to give himself up. At his trial, Butterworth was found guilty of manslaughter and sentenced to fifteen years' penal servitude.

Cowardly Killer

In late 1942 William Henry Turner, nineteen, deserted from the Army and went on the run. He relied on the goodness of the public and their belief that soldiers are always the good guys. On 29 December at 10 pm he arrived at the door of Rose Maria Cook who lived at Rookery House, Abbeygate, in Colchester. Mrs Cook let out rooms. Turner claimed to be a corporal and she gave him board in her son's room for the night. He repaid her kindness by stealing clothes and money. She immediately went to the police.

He moved to 48 North Hill, the home of Ida Ruth Walford and said that he was Corporal Swann. On Saturday, 2 January 1943, she went into his room and found a case had been broken into. She called the police and they arrived to arrest the thief. Charged, he was searched and money was found on him. Asked to explain the money, he said that he had killed a woman at 19 Audley Road in Colchester. He had knocked at the door and when no one answered pushed his way in. However, the house was not unoccupied. Ann Elizabeth Wade, an eighty-two-year-old, was at home and was bending over a chair when Turner entered unannounced. He later said that he put his arms around her and she 'just went limp'. He picked up the frail old lady and carried her to another room. Just then there was a knock at the door and a man asked for Miss Wade. Turner said that she had gone out and the man went away. Returning to Miss Wade, he found that she was now dead. He pushed her body under a bed, stole some money and left. He was charged with murder. Turner then claimed that he had been working for Miss Wade and had been playing around when she fell and died. His first trial ended in deadlock on 2 February. A second before the same judge, Mr Justice Asquith, found him guilty on 4 February and he was executed on 24 March 1943 by Thomas Pierrepoint, assisted by Henry Critchell at Pentonville.

Deserter-thief

Arthur Henry Jones was called up to the Army in March 1944

and stationed at Chelmsford. He was twenty-two years old. On 22 June, having served fewer than three months, Jones deserted after stealing some money from a locker belonging to one of his colleagues. He also took a Sten gun and two loaded magazines. Captain Samuel Grundy of the Home Guard met Jones near his headquarters at Bull Farm, near Abberton. Captain Grundy, 57, challenged Jones and a struggle ensued. Jones managed to free himself from the captain's grip and made off. For more than a quarter of a mile, Captain Grundy remained in pursuit, a pursuit that ended only when Jones shot him with the Sten gun. Immediately remorseful, Jones handed himself in to the police. At the trial, it was revealed that Jones had spent three weeks in a mental asylum for violent behaviour. The jury found him guilty of manslaughter and the judge sentenced Arthur Henry Jones to fifteen years' penal servitude.

Double Murder in Leigh-on-Sea

On 6 June 1945, Eva Rosemary Lucas, seventeen, returned to her home, Cranham in Undercliffe Gardens, Leigh-on-Sea, from a night out. She was horrified to find both her parents, Frederick Benjamin and Cissie Ciara Lucas, had been beaten to death. Police had no leads and it looked as if the crime would go into the files as yet another unsolved crime. Then a Mrs Wheeler of Morley Road, Barking, went to the police to report her suspicions about her forty-year-old brother, John Riley Young, who had been staying with her since 7 June, the day after the murders. He ran a jewellers shop in London and on the day he moved in with his sister, he paid £500 into a bank account in East Ham. That same afternoon he tried to commit suicide by slashing his wrists. Then he attempted to gas himself. Taken to hospital, the police went to question him. As they approached his bed, he said, 'I have been expecting you. It was me and I want to get it off my chest'. Found guilty at Chelmsford on 9 November, he was hanged by Albert Pierrepoint, assisted by Herbert Morris and Stephen Wade, at 8am on Friday 21 December 1945 at Pentonville.

Jealous Tommy Kills Pal

Sergeant James McNichol, thirty, was serving in the Heavy Anti-Aircraft Battery at Thorpe Bay at the end of the Second World War. On 16 August 1945, the day after VJ Day, McNichol and his girlfriend, Jean Neale, attended a dance in Chelmsford. The evening started off enjoyably for the couple but then she began flirting and dancing with some RAF men and two of McNichol's colleagues, Sergeants Donald Alfred Richard Kirkaldie and Leonard William Cox. McNichol flew into a rage and was still fuming later that night. Back at the Nissen hut shared by Kirkaldie, Cox and two others, one of the windows was smashed in the early hours of the next morning. A hand appeared through the broken pane and the light was switched on. Then a rifle appeared and shots rang out. Sergeant Cox was wounded but Sergeant Kirkaldie was hit in the throat and died immediately. McNichol was the prime suspect and arrested later that same day.

At his trial, which began on 13 November 1945, before Mr Justice Lewis, Jean Neale testified that she had only been out with McNichol on four occasions. On the night before the shooting, McNichol had asked her to go to an empty hut for a 'flirtation' but when she refused, he lost his temper. Realising that their relationship could not go on, Jean told McNichol that she was finished with him. The prosecution said that the ending of the affair was the final straw, but McNichol claimed that he had intended only to frighten Kirkaldie and Cox. The jury did not accept his plea and found him guilty of murder. On Friday, 21 December 1945, Albert Pierrepoint executed McNichol at Pentonville prison, assisted by Herbert Morris and Stephen Wade.

Killed for a Suit

In 1953 George James Newland was a young man in a hurry. Aged twenty-one, he fancied himself a good-looking man who would have more success in life and with the ladies if he looked the part. He determined that a new suit would help him achieve his goals. During his national service Newland was stationed in

Orsett where he was befriended by Henry and Honor Tandy, an elderly couple. Having been demobbed, Newland became a metal caster and returned to his home at Cogan Avenue, Walthamstow, east London, where he hatched a cruel idea. On 30 May 1953, he decided to visit the Tandys at their home in Grosvenor Road and took some apples and oranges with him – and also a claw hammer that he had taken from his father. The Tandys were pleased to see him and they spent some time chatting. Then Newland pulled out his hammer and attacked first Mrs Tandy and then her husband. Both suffered horrendous injuries and Mr Tandy, sixty-five, died in hospital. His wife later recovered from her wounds. Newland escaped with just £5 8s. At his trial before Mister Justice Streatfield at Chelmsford on 13 November 1953, Newland claimed that a violent film had influenced him. The jury found him guilty of murder. His appeal was dismissed on 7 December 1953 and Albert Pierrepoint, assisted by Harry Allen, hanged him at Pentonville on Wednesday, 23 December.

Sent Mad by Toyboy

On 20 February 1961, Albert Nickells, a forty-four-year-old charge hand at Ford's motor plant in Dagenham appeared at Essex Assizes. Although he loved his wife, his love was not enough and she left him for a young man. She agreed to see him but the thought of her and her lover sent him over the edge and he stabbed her twelve times before turning the knife on himself. At his trial he was found guilty of manslaughter and sentenced to three years in prison, the jury having taken his mental anguish into account.

Robbery Goes Horribly Wrong

Tea boy Brian Abbott appeared at Essex Assizes on 28 June 1962 accused of murdering forty-six-year-old Albert Crabb, the storeman at Abbott's former employers. Abbott had struck Mr Crabb with a hammer, robbed him of £15 and then set fire to his body. The sixteen-year-old was sentenced to be detained at Her Majesty's pleasure.

Index